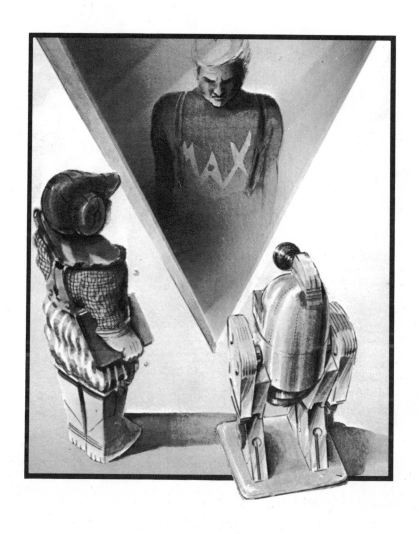

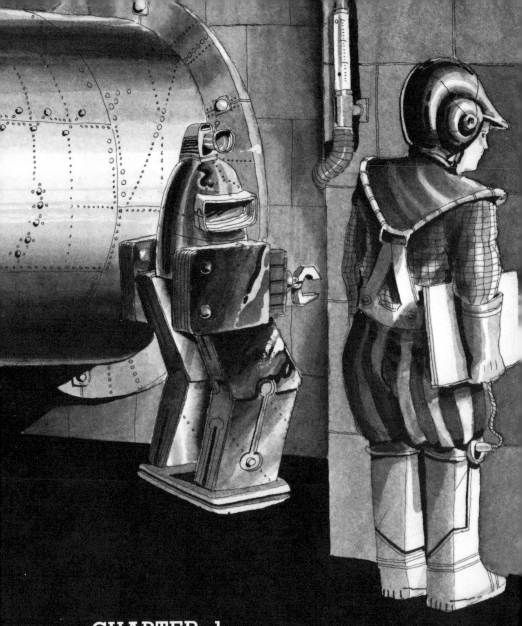

CHAPTER 1

Each day Todd did the same thing at his job.
He looked in the glass freezer room. It was his
job to make sure all of the bodies were still

Then he talked to Jeremy. Jeremy was a robot. He was also Todd's best friend.

Todd and Jeremy worked in a museum — in

"Just think. Some of the people in the freezer are a thousand years old," Todd said.

"Beep beep beep. I know that," Jeremy answered. "I know everything."

"I wonder what people were like back then," Todd said. "Let's hear you talk like a person from the 1990's."

Jeremy could do "voices." He could sound like any voice he had ever heard.

"OK, who is this?" Jeremy asked. Then he changed his voice. He talked like a President from the past. It was a game Jeremy and Todd always played.

"I don't know," Todd said. "But I'm going to ask a person who does!" He ran to the glass room.

"NO!" Jeremy called. He knew what Todd had in mind. But it was too late. In a few minutes, a man came out of the glass room. He was from the 1990's. He was tall and had a mean smile.

"Hello," Todd said. "Welcome to the 2990's. What was it like back in the 1990's? We would like to know."

"It was great," said the big man, "because everyone hated me!"

"Who are you?" Todd asked.

"I am Max Drackett — the most evil man who ever lived!"

6

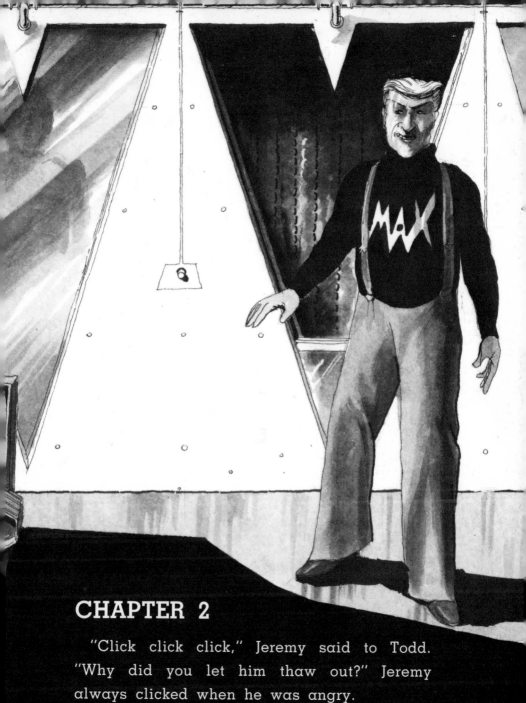

CHAPTER 2

"Click click click," Jeremy said to Todd. "Why did you let him thaw out?" Jeremy always clicked when he was angry.

"I thought he was a school teacher," Todd said. "That's what it said on his card."

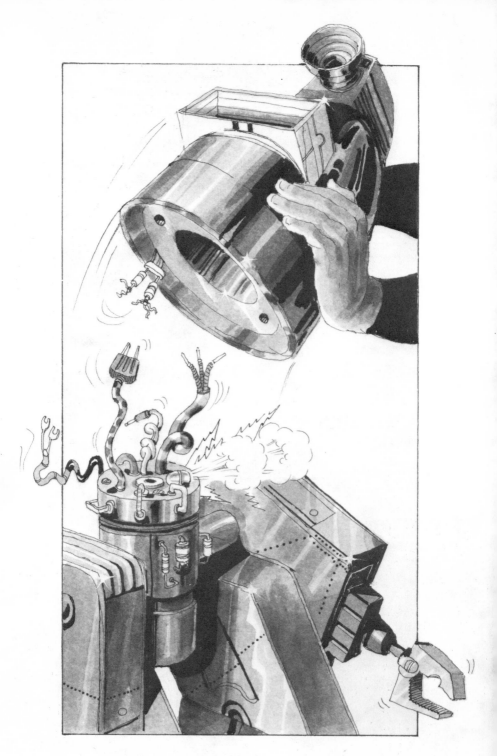

"Ha ha ha," Drackett laughed. "I changed the cards before I was frozen. I'm BAD news!"

Suddenly all of Jeremy's lights flashed on.

"Beep beep beep," Jeremy said.

"What is he doing?" Drackett asked Todd.

"He is thinking," Todd said.

"Beep beep beep," Jeremy began. "Max Drackett was the most evil man on Earth. He made his own rockets. Beep. He used them to blow things up. First he blew up all of Florida."

"I hate oranges!" Drackett explained.

"Beep beep beep. Here is the worst part," Jeremy went on. "Drackett hid some rockets. No one knows where. Right before he was frozen, he was going to . . ."

"Now I remember my greatest plan!" Drackett screamed. "I was going to blow up the world!"

"You can't do that," Todd said. "We are peaceful — not like you. No one ever fights now. We never have guns or war."

"Good!" Drackett laughed. "Then no one will stop me!" He grabbed Todd by the neck and pulled him toward the door. "You are coming with me," he said. "I must carry out my plan."

Jeremy started to follow them. So Drackett pulled Jeremy's head off!

"That should give us a head start!" Drackett laughed loudly.

CHAPTER 3

"What do you want with me?" Todd asked. Drackett was pushing him down the street

"You will show me around," Drackett said. "The world is different now. I don't know where anything is." But first Drackett wanted something to eat. He had not eaten in a long

"This is one of the places where we eat,"
Todd said. "We call them Fill-Ups."

"What will you have?" asked the girl behind
the counter.

"I'll have a cheeseburger," Drackett said.

"A cheeseburger!?" the girl laughed. "Have
you been sleeping for a thousand years?"

"Just give us the green tube," Todd said.

There were long tubes coming out of a ball.
The girl gave them green ones. They put

14

them in their mouths. The tubes filled them up
with food.

"That was awful!" Drackett said. "You people
should be blown up!" He pulled Todd out the
door.

Outside Todd thought about Jeremy. "I hope
Jeremy can fix his head," Todd thought. "And
then I hope he can find me!"

"Listen. Is there still a place called Yankee
Stadium?" Drackett asked.

"Sure. We saved it. It's part of our Big Park," Todd said. "The park has a zoo and a place for fish. A lot of people go there."

"Good!" Drackett laughed. "More people to blow up. Take me there!"

At Yankee Stadium Drackett found a secret

door in the ground.

"This is it!" he yelled. Then he saw a big pool of water. The sign said: DON'T FEED THE SHARKS!

"Well, that's it for you," Drackett said. And with that, he picked Todd up and threw him in.

CHAPTER 4

The sharks came closer and closer to Todd.

"Drackett is mean," Todd thought. "But he is not very smart. He didn't figure out that now sharks are peaceful too. They have become vegetarians."

Todd jumped out of the water. He ran back to

Yankee Stadium. Quickly Todd opened Drackett's secret door.

At first everything was dark. But pretty soon he could see. Carefully Todd felt his way down a hall. He came to a window. It looked down into a large, deep room.

19

And then he saw them — six silver rockets!

"I bet those things don't even work," Todd said out loud. "I bet Drackett gave up and went away." Todd kept talking to cover up the fact that he was scared.

Todd climbed down a ladder to get into the rocket room. Suddenly he heard a noise behind

him! Who was coming? There were feet on the
ladder.

"Click click, ouch!"

It was Jeremy!

"Jeremy! You are all right!" Todd said.

"Click, ouch. Click, ouch," Jeremy said.

Jeremy was not good at climbing ladders.

"It's a good thing you were wearing your radio," Jeremy said, "or I never would have found you. Even I didn't know where Drackett's secret room was. And I know everything."

Just then the door above the ladder closed with a bang.

"You know everything?" a voice laughed. "I bet you didn't know that I was going to trap you! Ha ha ha ha ha!"

Jeremy and Todd looked up. Drackett was at the window. He looked down at them and laughed. They were locked in!

CHAPTER 5

Drackett talked to them from the giant window. He spoke into a microphone.

"Soon the rockets will take off," Drackett said. "They will blow up the world. I have set

them for ten minutes. You will hear a voice count down your last few minutes on Earth! Ha ha ha ha!"

Todd and Jeremy looked around the room.

"There has got to be a button to turn the rockets off," Todd said.

Just then a computer voice spoke. "THE ROCKETS WILL TAKE OFF IN TEN MINUTES."

"I found it!" Todd yelled. He was pointing to a button close by.

"Well turn it off — fast!" Jeremy said.

Todd ran to the button. He pushed it. All the lights went out in the room.

"Wrong button. Click," Jeremy said.

"I don't need a robot to figure that out," Todd answered.

"THE ROCKETS WILL TAKE OFF IN EIGHT MINUTES," said the voice.

"Where is it?" Todd said. He started knocking things over to find the button. And all the time, Drackett watched and laughed.

"THE ROCKETS WILL TAKE OFF IN SEVEN MINUTES," said the voice.

Jeremy and Todd looked all over. But all they could find was the loudspeaker. Jeremy was holding it when the voice spoke.

"THE ROCKETS WILL TAKE OFF IN FOUR MINUTES."

"Beep, click. Not much time left," Jeremy said. "We will burn up when the rockets take off."

"Wait a minute!" Todd suddenly said. "I have got a plan. And I need your help!"

27

CHAPTER 6

"Listen to that voice," Todd told Jeremy.

"THE ROCKETS WILL TAKE OFF IN THREE MINUTES," said the voice from the speaker.

"Can you make your voice sound like that?" Todd asked. Jeremy said he could.

"Good," Todd said. "But say that there is only one minute left."

Todd waited for Drackett to turn his back. Then he pulled the wires out of the speaker.

"THE ROCKETS WILL TAKE OFF IN ONE MINUTE," Jeremy called out. He sounded just like the voice. Then he said, "THE ROCKETS WILL NOW TAKE OFF!"

But nothing happened! There were really two minutes left! Drackett waited for a second. Then he opened the door. He jumped down into the room.

"What happened? What went wrong?" Drackett screamed. He ran to the wall and opened a secret box. It had the button Jeremy and Todd were looking for.

"Jeremy! That's the button! Turn it off!" Todd yelled.

Jeremy stuck his hand in the wall. He broke the box into pieces.

"You can't do that!" Drackett said. He tried to pull Jeremy away. Electricity jumped through both of them. Drackett was knocked out cold.

Todd and Jeremy carried Drackett back to the museum. They were going to freeze him again.

"You can't go in right now," a guard said. "The power went out in the freezer room for a while. It's back on now, but all the people are running around loose. You have to wait till they freeze again."

Todd saw that Drackett was waking up.

31

"Where are you taking me?" Drackett asked. Todd had to think fast.

"Back to the Fill-Ups," Todd said.

"NO!" Drackett screamed. "Please freeze me again. Anything but the green tube!"

Todd and Jeremy smiled. They knew that their world was safe again.

CANON LAW FOR RELIGIOUS:

AN EXPLANATION

by

Joseph F. Gallen, S.J.

ALBA · HOUSE   NEW · YORK

SOCIETY OF ST. PAUL, 2187 VICTORY BLVD., STATEN ISLAND, NEW YORK 10314

Library of Congress Cataloging in Publication Data

Gallen, Joseph F.
  Canon law for religious.

  1. Canon law. 2. Monasticism and religious orders
(Canon law) I. Title.
LAW   262.9   83-15883
ISBN 0-8189-0461-5

Designed, printed and bound in the United States of
America by the Fathers and Brothers of the
Society of St. Paul, 2187 Victory Boulevard,
Staten Island, New York 10314, as part of their
communications apostolate.

---

2 3 4 5 6 7 8 9 (Current Printing: first digit)

CONTENTS

CHAPTER

INTRODUCTION

CANON LAW FOR RELIGIOUS is an explanation of the new canons on religious, promulgated by John Paul II, January 25, 1983 and effective from November 27 of the same year. It is concerned only with religious institutes and their members, not with secular institutes nor societies of apostolic life. The book is intended for all religious institutes but with the institutes of brothers, nuns and sisters very prominently in mind, especially as regards the practice of the Sacred Congregation for Religious and for Secular Institutes. The purpose is to explain the canons, not to advocate any position on the Church or religious institutes, whether conservative, moderate or liberal.

The canons are explained in their numerical order. Canons that wholly or in part are evident from a mere reading are not included. They can be found, as the text of all canons, in vernacular translations of at least the part of the code on religious. The Roman study group mentioned in the text is the one that compiled the canons on religious. Writings of mine in the *Review for Religious* and on canon law for religious in the preceding and present code, form a great part of this book. We are grateful to the *Review* for permission to reprint this matter. The following signs are used:

AAS *Acta apostolicae sedis*
CLD Bouscaren-O'Connor, *Canon Law Digest*
CLD 1980 Supplement. Supplement of the preceding.
CpR *Commentarium pro religiosis et missionariis*, Rome, 1920-
RfR *Review for Religious*, St. Louis, Mo., 1942-
SCRSI Sacred Congregation for Religious and for Secular Institutes

TPS *The Pope Speaks*
Vatican II Documents:
AA *Decree on the Apostolate of the Laity*
CD *Decree on the Bishops' Pastoral Office in the Church*
GES *Constitution on the Church in the Modern World*
LG *Dogmatic Constitution on the Church*
PC *Decree on the Appropriate Renewal of Religious Life*
PO *Decree on the Ministry and Life of Priests*
ES *Ecclesiae sanctae, Norms for the Implementation of Some Decrees of the Council*

Rev. Joseph F. Gallen, S.J.
Jesuit Community
St. Joseph's University
5600 City Ave.
Philadelphia, PA 19131

CANON LAW FOR RELIGIOUS

CHAPTER I

NORMS COMMON TO ALL INSTITUTES OF CONSECRATED LIFE

Institutes of consecrated life are divided into religious and secular institutes (cann. 573-730). These are approximated by societies of apostolic life. Chapter I of this work applies to both religious and secular institutes, the remaining chapters only to religious institutes.

573, § 1. *Consecrated Life in General.* The first canon states the nature and purpose of a consecrated life in general. Consecration separates one from the purely temporal, secular and profane, and devotes him/her to divine and eternal things. This, in the concrete, is principally a striving for the perfection of the practice of the supreme, infused and theological virtue of charity, by which we love God above all things for himself and ourselves and the neighbor for the love of God (Royo, *Teologia della perfezione cristiana*, no. 254).

This life can therefore be best summarized as one of universal and total supernatural love. The original consecration to such a life is by baptism, by which charity is infused. The evangelical counsels intensify charity (LG, no. 44) by controlling the principal obstacles to perfect love: the divided heart, by *chastity* (1 Cor 7:33); the fascination for material things, by *poverty*; an inordinate self-love, or pride, by *obedience* (Ph 2:8, Rm 5:19). The love of intensified charity is directed primarily to God, consequently to the neighbor, and thus extends to the salvation of mankind, to the service of the Church, the kingdom of God on earth. It makes its possessor an outstanding sign in the Church, whose mission is the eternal salvation of mankind, and a manifestation of the glory of heaven. Eternal glory is effected by the perfect possession of God, and God is love (1 Jn 4:16). This life is lived in act by living Christ personally and totally.

§ 2. Such a form of life is to be lived in all institutes of the consecrated states. Their foundation is preeminently a spiritual and supernatural work and thus implies the illumination and inspiration of the Holy Spirit. A person in law is the subject of rights and obligations. By baptism an individual is incorporated into the Church and becomes a member, the subject of rights and obligations. There are also juridical persons in the Church, as in the civil state, e.g., corporations. These likewise are, as such, the subjects of rights and obligations which are distinct from the rights and obligations of the individuals that compose them.

In canon law these were called moral persons; in the new canon law, they are styled as juridical persons. For example, an institute, province or house of the consecrated life becomes capable of acquiring, administering and owning temporal goods by its erection as a juridical person. The act of incorporation into any institute of consecrated life is a profession to observe the three evangelical counsels. The precise nature of the act of incorporation may be by vows or other sacred bonds similar to vows, according to the law of the particular institute. However, in a religious institute the temporary and perpetual bond must be by public vows.

574, § 1. *Consecrated States Appertain to the Sanctity of the Church.* The canon declares that the consecrated life appertains to the life and holiness of the Church, which is evident. The general purpose of the consecrated life is to strive for the perfection of charity in Christ, which is sanctity. The primary purpose of the apostolate, whether direct in apostolic institutes, or indirect by prayer, austerity and witnessing to Christ in contemplative institutes, is to lead others to sanctity of life. The canon affirms the evident principle that this life should be promoted and favored by all in the Church.

§ 2. *Special Vocation and Purpose.* A special call or invitation from God is necessary for the consecrated life. This is termed a divine vocation. What is meant is an interior illumination and inspiration of the Holy Spirit that entrance into the consecrated life is the will of God for the particular person. It is an invitation or counsel, not a command of God. The purpose is that those in the consecrated life "may have a special role in the Church and contribute to its salvific mission," which is contained in the first canon.

575. *Origin of the Evangelical Counsels.* Consecrated life is a total and radical living of Christ. As he was chaste, poor and obedient, so is the consecrated person. Chastity is counseled in Mt 19:10-12; 1 Cor 7:7-9, 32-8 and in LG, no. 42; poverty in Mt 19:21-4; 13:22; Lk 12:34 and obedience in Ph 2:8, Rm 5:19, and PC, no. 14. Since the evangelical counsels are part of revealed truth and since institutes of consecrated life are ecclesiastical juridical persons, and their members baptized persons, it is evident that the authority of the Church extends to the evangelical counsels, to such institutes and to their members.

576. "Church authority has the duty, under the inspiration of the Holy Spirit, of interpreting these evangelical counsels, of regulating their practice, and finally of establishing stable forms of living according to them" (LG, no. 43) ". . . it devolves on the same hierarchy to govern with wise legislation the practice of the evangelical counsels" (*ibid.*, no. 45) "Submissively following the promptings of the Holy Spirit, the hierarchy endorses rules formulated by eminent men and women and authentically approves later modifications. Moreover, by its watchful and shielding authority, the hierarchy keeps close to communities established far and wide for the upbuilding of Christ's body, so that they can grow and flourish in accord with the spirit of their founders" (*ibid.*, no. 45).

578. *Principal Responsibility is to Live the Vocation of the Institute.* According to this canon, the fundamental obligation of every institute is to know its vocation in Christ and in the Church. Paul VI and Vatican II insisted often that the true vocation of an institute of consecrated life was, "fidelity to its origin," "the complete mentality of their founder remains and inspires the members," "the most genuine faithfulness to the origins of your institute" (RfR, 35 [1976], 131-3); "acknowledge

and preserve the spirit of the founders and all the particular goals and wholesome traditions which constitute the heritage of each institute" (PC, no. 2); "a true knowledge of their original spirit" (ES, II, no. 16). The essential vocation of a particular institute is therefore centered in fidelity to its origin, to the mind and spirit of its founder, and to its legitimate traditions, all with relation to the life and work. These traditions can have arisen subsequent to the origin of an institute. It is a regrettable fact that a synthesis of the essential vocation as a particular institute is found in remarkably few constitutions of the past.

The important document of the SCRSI and the Sacred Congregation for Bishops, May 14, 1978, on *the Relations between Bishops and Religious*, describes the charism of founders:

"The 'charism of the founders' seems to be a certain experience of the Spirit which they pass on to their disciples so that the latter may live in accordance with it and preserve, deepen and constantly intensify it as the body of Christ grows ceaselessly. Hence 'the Church cherishes and fosters the distinctive character of the different religious institutes.' The distinctive character also entails a special style of sanctification and apostolate. This style, in turn, creates a tradition specific to each so that its objective components can be readily ascertained. . . .

"Any authentic charism brings with it a certain element of genuine newness for the spiritual life of the Church, as well as a special power of energetic activity, which may well seem out of place to those around and which can even be a source of difficulties since it is not easy to recognize immediately its origin in the Spirit.

"The charismatic note distinctive of each institute requires that both the founder and his disciples continuously test their fidelity to the Lord, their docility to his Spirit, their prudent attention to circumstances and careful analysis of the signs of the times, their determination to be an organic part of the Church, their consciousness of obedience to the sacred hierarchy, their intrepidity in carrying out their undertakings, their constancy in sacrificing themselves and their humility in suffering adversity. A proper relationship between a genuine charism, new perspectives and interior trials brings with it an unbroken historical link between the charism and the cross. This connection, unaccompanied by any effort to justify rejection and misunderstanding, is very useful for discerning whether or not a vocation is authentic'' (TPS, 23 [1978], 352-3).'

Under another heading, the sacred congregations give norms for evaluating the charism of a founder:

''a) It originates solely in the Spirit as something distinct, even if not separated from innate and acquired personal endowments that manifest themselves in doing and organizing.

b) There is a profound desire of the soul to become like Christ in order to bear witness to some aspects of his mystery.

c) There is a fruitful love for the Church that unconditionally avoids stirring any dissent within it.

In addition, if founders are to be authentically such, they must be men and women whose tested virtue shows sincere docility to the sacred hierarchy and to the inspiration that persists in them as a gift of the Spirit'' (*ibid.*, 373).

All of the sources given above evidently favor a sound renewal and adaptation according to Vatican II. Obviously also all constitutions or principal codes should contain a synthesis of the charism or spirit of the particular institute.

579. *Erection of Institutes.* Institutes of consecrated life were described above under can. 573, § 2. As soon as they are validly erected, they and their members are the subjects of the laws, of the rights and of the obligations enacted for these institutes and their members. Obviously the Roman Pontiff is competent to erect a new institute (can. 589). Canon 579 states that the competent authorities are diocesan bishops in their own territory. This phrase does not preclude the diffusion of the diocesan institute into other dioceses. The same power is to be attributed to the heads of other particular churches likened to dioceses in law, such as a

territorial prelature or abbey, a vicariate apostolic, or a prefecture apostolic, as well as apostolic administrations stably erected.

Formal Decree. The erection of the new diocesan institute is to be made by a formal decree. The decree should be in writing, and a copy of it is to be kept in both the institute and the diocese. The bishop is also obliged to inform the sacred congregation of his act of erecting the institute and to send a copy of the decree to the sacred congregation, in which he is to take special care that the title, nature and purpose of the particular institute are explicitly and exactly defined.

Previous Consultation of the Apostolic See is Required. This recourse is ordinarily to the SCRSI but if the institute is founded in the missions and principally working there recourse is had to the S. Congregation for the Evangelization of Nations, formerly called only the S. Congregation for the Propagation of the Faith. Before consulting these, the bishop may and will in fact have to permit a private and imperfect beginning of community life and of the works of the apostolate according to the nature of the proposed institute. This experiment is factually necessary for the judgment of all the authorities as to whether a group should be erected into a diocesan institute. It would be more prudent for the diocesan bishop to consult the sacred congregation even before this experiment is begun. The founding of an institute is not a frequent event in a diocese, and a bishop can receive useful information and guidance by such a recourse. In the formal consultation of the sacred congregation to erect a diocesan institute, a bishop should give information such as that listed as of 1970 in O'Connor, *Canon Law Digest*, vol. 7, p. 458, which is as follows:

The following document is given without specific date as issued by the S. C. for Religious and Secular Institutes. It carries the heading: "documents to be sent in for the erection of a group into a congregation of diocesan law or to obtain a decree of praise."

1. Name and surname in the world and in religion of the founder or foundress as well as of the first superior or superioress general together with a short sketch of their lives.

2. A historico-juridical report of the group from its beginning.

3. Two copies of its book of prayers, its book of ceremonies, and its book of customs, if such are in use among the membership.

4. Photographs of the religious habit for the novices and for the professed.

5. Six copies of the text of the constitutions drawn up for it as an institute of diocesan law or as an institute of pontifical law.

6. Numerical prospectus (statistics) of the members and of the houses of the group; if they are diffused through many dioceses, the ordinaries of those dioceses should be instructed to send testimonials directly to this S. Congregation.

7. Declaration on the following points:

(a) At the foundation of the group or in its history have there been extraordinary events such as visions and the like?

(b) What special devotions and what special exercises of piety are given preference?

(c) Is there in the diocese another institute with the same name and with the same special purpose?

Furthermore, the sum of 150 U.S. dollars should be sent to this S. Department for the necessary expenses which, when the business is completed, will be defined in detail.

Above all, the reasons for and against such an erection should accurately be given. All other pertinent information should be included, e.g., the means of support of the proposed institute. The diocesan bishop should present six copies of the constitutions at this time. He should also request from the sacred congregation the faculties that may be necessary during the early years of the institute, e.g., of appointing the first general superior, general councilors, general treasurer, and general secretary; of admitting to and receiving the vows or other bond of the first general superior and the other members; of dispensing from some canonical laws, e.g., of counting the time in the preceding experimentation as the noviceship or of dispensing from it in whole or in part so that some members may make profession immediately.

It would be well to conclude these requests with a petition for the other faculties that the sacred congregation considers necessary or opportune. I myself now believe that it would be better and more practical to initiate an apostolic institute also with governmental structure of an autonomous house. This is more in conformity with the number of the group at the time and is more apt to prevent the imprudent admission of candidates, which is a strong temptation at the beginning of a centralized institute. The autonomous structure should be changed to that of a centralized apostolic institute when a sufficient number of members has been attained. (The former can. 492, § 3, forbidding a new institute to assume the same name or habit as an institute already established, has not been retained in the new canon law).

580. *Aggregation to Another Institute.* Aggregation is an act by which an institute is authoritatively admitted and recognized as a moral member of the third consecrated order or institute. The effect of the aggregation is that the institute obtains the spiritual favors, e.g., indulgences, and the liturgical privileges granted to the first and second orders. The aggregated institute is in no way subject to the authority or ecclesiastical power of governing of the first order and in no way participates in its juridical privileges, e.g., exemption.

A prerequisite of aggregation is that the aggregated institute have some similarity with the first order in spirit, manner of life, and also in the habit and title. However, the last condition is not rigorously exacted. Aggregation is made by the competent superior of the first order or institute. An aggregation at the erection of an institute takes effect only when the diocesan bishop has given the formal decree of erection. Aggregation may be made by the competent superiors of all institutes that have the privilege of granting aggregation, e.g., Friars Minor, Conventuals, Capuchins, Dominicans, Augustinians, Carmelites, Servites, and Benedictines.

581. *Constitution and Change of Parts of an Institute.* The canon merely states that all such actions appertain to the authority of an institute determined in the constitutions, whether the institute is clerical or lay, pontifical or diocesan. It has not been the practice to erect an institute into provinces before it became pontifical. The canon must intend true

parts, which have been at least almost universally termed provinces in the past.

Province. The understanding of a province is that of a distinct juridical person, composed of at least three canonically erected houses, governed by a superior distinct from the local and general superior, and who possesses ordinary authority, i.e., authority given by law and not merely by delegation from a higher superior. If a part of an institute verifies this definition, it is a province and subject to all the common law norms on provinces, no matter by what name it may be designated in the particular constitutions.

The practice of the SCRSI has usually required also that an institute be capable of division into at least three provinces and that the total number of members in each province be at least one hundred. Other divisions of an institute, such as vice-provinces, can verify the definition and be true provinces, differing only in such extrinsic matters as number, e.g., three hundred religious being required for a province, and concerning the number of elected delegates to the general chapter, e.g., a vice-province having only one delegate and a province two.

Canon law does not demand that each province have its own house of formation, e.g., a novitiate and a house of studies. It has been at least the ordinary understanding that a province should be soon self-sufficient financially and in personnel. A modern factor such as nationalism can require that a region or mission be erected into a province even though lacking this self-sufficiency. The provincial superior of the former province should then continue to assist the new province by money and members. The general chapter or general superior may oblige other provinces and even the entire institute to assist such a new province.

Regions. This is the more recent general term for parts of an institute that are not distinct juridical persons and consequently are not provinces. In particular institutes such divisions have various names, e.g., vice-provinces, quasi-provinces, missions, districts, provincial or general commissariats. In the recent practice of the SCRSI, the authority of the regional superior must be delegated, not ordinary (RfR, 33 [1974], 1501-2).

Since the regional superior is governing on the intermediate level, the authority delegated to him is very commonly the same in extent and degree as that of a provincial superior. The norm in the constitutions for the authority competent to establish, change or disestablish regions should be the same as that given below for provinces. Since his authority is delegated, not ordinary, the regional superior is not a major superior. The authority also will usually be delegated by the general superior or chapter, but in a region dependent on a province, it may be delegated by a provincial superior according to the constitutions.

Houses Immediately Dependent on the General Superior. Some houses may be assigned to no province but made immediately subject to the general superior, e.g., the general motherhouse and some distant houses, such as those of a mission, as also houses of formation. Provision should be made for all such houses with regard to the general chapter, e.g., that one or two delegates elected by the entire group of these houses will be members of the general chapter.

Sufficient Reasons for Division into Provinces. The common reason for this division is that the institute cannot be properly governed by the one higher superior because of its large number of members, wide territorial diffusion, or both. Diversity of country or language or of both among the members is also a frequent factor.

The acts contemplated in the canon are the original division into provinces, the erection of additional provinces, modification of boundaries, and the union of provinces. The particular constitutions may determine the authority for these ''supraprovincial'' acts by giving it to the general superior with the consent of his council or to the general chapter when in session, otherwise to the general superior with the consent of his council. The consent should be demanded because of the importance of the matter.

582. *All Federations, Mergers, and Unions of Consecrated Life are Reserved to the Apostolic See Alone.* This principle therefore includes a union in which the autonomy of the components is preserved, whether these are distinct institutes, autonomous monasteries, or federations of autonomous monasteries, thus resulting in a confederation; also a union

by which an autonomous monastery or institute is absorbed by another, or is united to form a third and distinct monastery or institute from the components (RfR, 27 [1968], 549-51). The separation of some members to constitute a new institute is also reserved to the Holy See (see RfR especially 35 [1976], 79-80, 131-33, and 36 [1977], 139-40). The establishment of associations, a diversified form of federation, of monasteries of nuns is also reserved to the Holy See.

583. *Changes Affecting Matters Approved by the Holy See.* These matters may not be changed, even in a diocesan institute, except with the approval of the Holy See, e.g., the title, special end and works.

584. *Suppression of an Institute.* Suppression is the authoritative withdrawal of the character of a juridical person from an institute, province or house, or of the approval of a separated establishment or filial house.

Any suppression of an institute, even if it is only indirect and implicit and if the institute consists of only one house and is diocesan, is reserved to the Holy See. The disposition of the property of a supressed institute is also reserved to the Holy See. The property of the individual members, e.g., the dowries, will be restored to them. The Holy See determines in each suppression the state of the former members, by granting a dispensation from the vows or a transfer to another institute.

585. *Suppression of a Part (Province).* The suppression of a part of an institute and the disposition of its property appertain to the authority determined by its proper law. As was said of erection, these acts may be assigned to the general superior with the consent of his council or to the general chapter when in session. Again the consent should be required because of the importance of the matter. The same authority may be enacted regarding the disestablishment of regions.

586. *Autonomy of Life.* The canon states that a just autonomy of life, especially of government, is to be recognized for each institute. Apparently the internal life of an institute is primarily intended here, i.e., the relation of members to the superiors of the institute, the constitutions or principal code, the directory or statutes, and the proper law in general, as also the charism, spirit, nature, character, sound traditions of an institute, and its doctrinal, spiritual and liturgical heritage. The canon de-

clares that it appertains to bishops to protect and foster this autonomy.
587. §§ 1, 3. *Constitutions*.

a) *Rule*. Rule in the singular signifies the fundamental and immutable law given by ancient founders and approved by the Church. The most famous Rules are those of St. Basil, St. Augustine, St. Benedict, and St. Francis of Assisi. The Rule of St. Basil is used by religious of the Oriental Church, that of St. Augustine also by Dominican and Ursuline nuns and in the many institutes of Dominican sisters, that of St. Francis in the many institutes of Franciscan nuns, sisters and brothers, that of St. Benedict in the many institutes of Benedictine sisters. All of these ancient Rules are composed of spiritual principles. They consequently had to be complemented by juridical articles and also statutes that would adapt the Rule to the specific purpose, works, and government of a particular institute. These additions were commonly called ''Constitutions.''

In the modern sense, Constitutions signify the primary and fundamental law of an institute. Even in institutes that have one of the ancient Rules, the Constitutions are ordinarily as complete and the same as in institutes that have no Rule. When used in the plural and in the modern sense, rules mean the more detailed enactments of the institute in general or those for particular classes, e.g., rules for novices, scholastics, brothers, local superiors and teachers. According to the present canon, the term ''fundamental code'' is used by some institutes instead of ''constitutions.'' Recently some institutes have begun to use ''constitution'' in the singular.

b) *Excessive Amount of Canon Law in the Constitutions*. The remedy is simply to omit canon law in the constitutions and directory. It is evident that the new canon law will very soon be translated into at least the principal vernacular languages. Handbooks of the canons on the consecrated life can also be compiled in the vernacular; several have been so compiled in the last few years. Some canonists seem to fear this and to insist, without determining them, that the principal canons should be retained in the constitutions. A canon should be retained to the extent that it is necessary for the complete sense of a section or an article of the constitutions or directory; otherwise it should be omitted. The canons themselves can be found in another book and in the vernacular. Obviously the authoritative guide in this matter will be the instructions and practice of the SCRSI.

c) *Constitutions.* The constitutions are made up of two types of articles; the more important juridical norms of the institute and the more important spiritual principles of the consecrated life and of the particular institute. It seems evident enough that the spiritual articles should be drawn primarily from the basic truths of spiritual theology, the headings of which are listed, in great part from Vatican II, in the article, *Typical Constitutions*, RfR, 34 (1975), 194-7. The spiritual articles are to be written in more of a personal and inspiring rather than in a flat and abstract manner. The matter of these articles is to be solid, not mere devotionalism nor a few random thoughts on various virtues.

The spiritual articles may be proposed as the introductory articles of several chapters. They may also be interweaved with the juridical text. Either of these forms appears to be more favored and demanded by the SCRSI. I myself favor the separation of the articles, the first part of the constitutions being spiritual, the second juridical. This makes the spiritual content easier to use for spiritual reading, reflection, and mental prayer. It also avoids the danger of the juridical articles drying up the spiritual. There will be very little occasion for a spiritual content in the directory.

An easy way to make a beginning of the juridical articles is to study the same article cited in the preceding paragraph. I now believe that only the substantive or essential articles on the general chapter should be in the constitutions and placed before the articles on the general superior. The rest of the chapter articles should be placed at the end of the directory. These substantive articles are the convocation, an adequate listing of the members and the manner of the election of delegates, the president, the purpose, the essentials of the manner of electing general and provincial superiors and officials, the members of the provincial chapter, its purpose, the number and manner of electing the delegates, whether it has the power of making enactments, the confirmation of these and elections, the frequency of the provincial chapter and its president.

There is also in the RfR, 38 (1979), 71-7, an unofficial publication of an outline of the matter to be contained in the constitutions for the guidance of officials and consultors of the SCRSI. It is helpful but by no means adequate. For example, it mentions only once matter which might appertain to the directory rather than the constitutions. The distinction of the matter for each of these is new and is one of the present problems in compiling constitutions.

Can. 587, § 1 lists the juridical matters to be contained in the constitutions, in addition to the matter in can. 578, "the fundamental norms on the government of the institute and the discipline of the members, their incorporation and formation, as also the proper objects of the sacred bonds." The SCRSI apparently holds the same principle for the articles on dismissal and for the more important articles on temporal administration.

d) *Directory*. This name has thus far been the favorite one chosen for this part of proper law. It may be called "Statutes" or designated by any other suitable name. The SCRSI has as yet given no official listing of what should be in the directory as opposed to the constitutions. In my own reflection and work, I have concluded that details, matters that do not touch the usual life and formalities, constitute the context of the directory. These were listed in the RfR article, *Writing Constitutions*, 36 (1977), 778-9, as follows:

(1) *Details*. Description of the religious habit; clothes and accessories to be brought by those entering; sum for the expenses of the noviceship; length of annual retreat and of that before the noviceship and profession; details and circumstances regarding religious exercises, cloister, correspondence, silence, community life, formation, apostolate, care of the sick and aged, suffrages for the dead; details on the office of the general superior; listing of matters that require the deliberative or consultative vote of councils on the general, provincial, regional, and local levels; that require confirmation, approval, or consent of a higher authority; details on the offices of general secretary and treasurer,

provincials and local superiors, councils and officials, on houses, local assistants and local councils, the director and assistant director of novices.

(2) *Matters That do not Touch the Usual Life.* Among these are devotional renewal of vows, making and change of the cession of administration of personal property, disposal of its use and income, making of a will and its change, profession of a novice in danger of death, and lesser norms on the administration of the temporal goods of an institute.

(3) Detailed norms on precedence; record of property brought by candidates; signed statement from candidates that they will not seek compensation from the institute if they leave, are excluded or dismissed; entrance testimonials of baptism, confirmation, of good moral character, health, and other testimonials for admission; written and signed declaration of profession (see also *Typical Constitutions*, RfR, 34 [1975], 213-27).

(4) *Custom Book.* This has contained lesser norms but below the level of those now to be placed in the directory or statutes, e.g., details on secondary employments not connected with government, such as the cook, refectorian, infirmarian, sacristan; on the quality and form of clothing; the quality of food; details on the practice of poverty, of the different exercises, recreation, observance of feasts and similar matters. I believe that the duties of officials such as those just mentioned should be typed and a copy given to the official. This should be done for such other offices as that of archivist. I see no reason for including particular office or job descriptions in a book of norms.

§ 2. e). *Approval and Change of Constitutions and Directory.* The constitutions and any change in them of a pontifical institute must be approved by the SCRSI. There are some constitutions, even though not many, that were not approved by the Holy See, and these may be changed without its permission (see Maroto, CpR [1937], 250-3 and Larraona, *ibid.*, 4 [1923], 137-9). The same approvals for a diocesan institute appertain to the bishop of the principal house, which is the generalate, but all other diocesan bishops are to be consulted, if the institute has been extended to many dioceses (can. 595, § 1).

§ 4. f) *Other Books*. The same approvals with regard to the directory appertain to the general chapter. The general superior, with the consent of his council, may interpret, add, change, or abrogate particular sections of the directory, but the general revision should be reserved to the general chapter. The possible part of the general superior just stated depends on the practice of the SCRSI in approving constitutions, and is put forth here as a possibility, not as something officially confirmed. The same norms may be applied to older books such as books of rules, custom books, ceremonials and books of community prayers, although greater authority over custom books could be given to the general and other major superiors.

g) *Authentic Interpretation*. The same authority as in e) above is required for the authentic interpretation of pontifical and diocesan constitutions. Such an interpretation has the force of law and consequently may be given only by the legislator or his delegate (can. 16). A doctrinal interpretation is one given by canonical authors on constitutions in general or of those of a particular institute. As a purely private interpretation, it possesses only the weight and value of the arguments on which it rests.

In a doubt about the sense of any matter of proper law, the superior may determine what observance is to be followed. This is in effect a regulation of the superior. Outside of an urgent case, such an interpretation appertains to higher superiors. The general chapter is the interpreter of the directory and its own enactments as also those of previous chapters and, outside a general chapter, also the general superior. Each superior may authentically interpret his own regulations and a higher superior may do so also with regard to those of a lower superior. It is also evident that only the Holy See may authentically interpret or change the canonical laws and its own decrees, whether these are contained in the constitutions or not.

588, § 2. *Clerical and Lay Institutes*. Institutes of consecrated life may be either clerical or lay. An institute is *clerical* if by its purpose or design intended by the founder or by legitimate tradition it is under the direction of clerics, assumes the exercise of sacred orders and is recognized as clerical by the authority of the Church. The assumption of sacred orders by a few members merely for the houses of the institute would not enter into the purpose or equivalent design of an institute. The Church authority competent for clerical recognition is not restricted to the Holy See and therefore extends also to diocesan bishops.

§ 3. An Institute is *lay* that is recognized as such by the authority of the Church, and by its nature, character or purpose has a distinctive function that does not include the exercise of sacred orders.

Vatican II declared: "This sacred Synod declares that there is no objection to religious congregations of brothers admitting some members to Holy Orders, to supply needed priestly ministrations for their own houses, provided that the lay character of the congregation remains unchanged and that it is the general chapter that makes the decision" (PC, no. 10).

589. *Definitions of Pontifical and Diocesan Institutes.* An institute is pontifical if erected as an institute by the Holy See or approved by it as pontifical after its erection as an institute by a diocesan bishop. If an institute erected in the latter way has not obtained an approval as pontifical from the Apostolic See, it is diocesan. Apparently there will be one approbation in the future, not both a decree of praise and of definitive approval as in the past. Neither the preceding nor the present canon law requires the permission of a diocesan bishop to become pontifical. The list of requirements for becoming pontifical has been given above under can. 579.

The primary requisite for obtaining pontifical approval is that the institute have proved its stability and its worth by the consecrated lives of its members and the fruitfulness of its apostolate. These facts are established primarily by the attestations of the diocesan bishops. It is not necessary that the institute have houses in more than one diocese. It is to be noted that in the list under can. 579 the previous approval of the constitutions by the diocesan bishop is not required for the attainment of pontifical status.

590. *Subjection to Supreme Authority.* Institutes of consecrated life are

particularly subject to the supreme authority in the Church as public associations of distinctive rights and obligations in the Church, especially also from their nature and purpose of striving for sanctity of life in an ecclesial manner and their dedication to the apostolate of the whole Church. The Roman Pontiff is considered an internal superior. He is the first and highest superior of every institute and of all its members. As an internal superior, he may command in virtue of the bond of obedience, but this is a power he almost never uses. The pope in fact governs institutes by his ecclesiastical power of government, which he exercises by the laws of the code of canon law, especially those dealing exclusively with the consecrated state, and the decrees of the Holy See. Most of the later emanate from the SCRSI.

The ordinary government of the consecrated states by the Holy See is exercised by the SCRSI through instructions, decrees, private replies to questions, petitions and reports, and through the examination, correction and approval of constitutions and of their revisions. ''Religious institutes founded in the missions and principally working there; societies of ecclesiastics and women without vows'' are subject to the Sacred Congregation for the Evangelization of Nations.

Consecrated states and their members are subject to the other Roman congregations, tribunals and offices in their respective fields. Individuals may recur directly to the Holy See. Institutes recur ordinarily through their own general procurator or through that of another institute; through the diocesan bishop, especially of the motherhouse; through an approved agent in Rome, even if he is a secular; or through an ecclesiastic in Rome known to the Roman Curia. An institute should always strive to obtain the original or an identical copy of a document directed to it by the Holy See and should also retain this in its files.

591. *Exempt, Pontifical and Diocesan Institutes*. Can. 591 states that the Roman Pontiff may exempt institutes of consecrated life from the jurisdiction of the local Ordinaries and subject them to himself alone or to another ecclesiastical authority for the good of the institutes, the needs of the apostolate, or the common good. No criterion is given by which exempt institutes can be determined but it is to be presumed that the

institutes thus far exempt will retain this exemption. In virtue of the previous can. 615 all orders were exempt, provided in the case of orders of women that they were subject to an order of men.

Practically all monasteries of nuns of simple vows were not exempt in fact. Congregations, institutes of simple vows, were not exempt unless they had obtained this privilege by a special indult from the Holy See, e.g., the Passionists and Redemptorists. Congregations of brothers and sisters were not exempt. The bishop may make a visitation of the members and houses of pontifical religious institutes only in the cases expressed in law (can. 397, § 2). Religious may be punished by the local ordinary even with penalties in all matters in which they are subject to him. For an urgent and most serious reason, a diocesan bishop may forbid a member of an institute of consecrated life to remain in the diocese, if the latter's higher superior has been warned of but neglected to take care of the case. The matter is to be immediately reported to the Holy See (can. 679).

By can. 586, § 1 all institutes possess a just autonomy of life, especially of government, and their own proper discipline. By can. 594 a diocesan institute is under the special care of a diocesan bishop. The bishop of the principal house approves the constitutions of a diocesan institute and confirms changes made in them (can. 595, § 1), as explained under can. 587. This bishop may not confirm changes in constitutions in matters on which the Apostolic See (can. 595, § 1) had already placed its hands, which had already been reserved to the Holy See concerning all institutes by can. 583. He also handles major matters affecting the whole institute that exceed the power of internal authority. He is to consult all other diocesan bishops in the matters above if the institute has been extended to many dioceses (can. 595, § 1). Autonomous monasteries of nuns are also under the special vigilance of the diocesan bishop (can. 615).

In virtue of can. 595, § 2, a diocesan bishop as such can give dispensations from the constitutions of a diocesan institute but not from the common laws contained in them. His power of dispensing is restricted to particular cases. He may therefore dispense both individuals and, with safe probability, also houses, provinces or an entire institute for a sufficiently general reason and for as long as this reason exists. The particular or special character of a dispensation is verified not only when it is given to an individual but also when granted for a special, accidental and transitory necessity to a house, province or institute.

Law in the Consecrated Life

a) *Excuse*. An excuse from the observance of a law means that the obligation simply ceases to exist for a subject of a law. No one may place an action that is intrinsically evil, for example, blasphemy, idolatry, denial of the faith, hatred of God, and so forth. The obligation of other laws generally ceases when an accidental but special difficulty, disproportionate to the observance of the law, is connected with its observance; for example, it is impossible for one in a weak and dying condition to attend Sunday mass. In an excuse the obligation simply ceases to exist of itself; there is no need of a relaxing of the obligation, which is a dispensation, or of a declaration by an ecclesiastical authority or a superior.

b) *Permission*. Some laws do not forbid an act absolutely but only when it is done without the permission of a competent superior. For example, both the past and present canon law forbid alienation of ecclesiastical property above a determined value without the permission of the Holy See, as also the administration of property belonging to lay persons by clerics or religious without the permission of their own ordinary. The permission makes the act licit, and the law is observed. Permission does not remove the obligation and free from the observance of the law, as is done in a dispensation. A permission, in general, is granted for lesser reasons than a dispensation. It may also be presumed, unless formal and express permission is demanded by a particular law. A dispensation may not be presumed, because the obligation of a law ceases by a dispensation only through the actual exercise of the dispensing power.

c) *Dispensation*. A dispensation is the liberation from the obligation of a law in a special case, granted by competent authority for a proportionate reason. The act of the competent authority frees from the obligation. The case is special because the law remains; a dispensation is not the abrogation of a law but the authoritative liberation from its obligation. It may be granted by those who possess executive power, within the limits of their competency, and also by those who have the power explicitly or implicitly of dispensing either from law itself or by reason of legitimate delegation (can. 85).

A sufficient reason is required for liceity when a dispensation is granted by the legislator or his superior but for validity in a dispensation granted by an inferior. The reason or reasons should be proportionate to the gravity of the law in question. They evidently need not be as serious as those required for an excuse but they should at least be such as to make the observance of the law more than ordinarily difficult or onerous or render the observance of the law obstructive of a greater good. A dispensation may be licitly asked or given in a doubt about the sufficiency of a reason (can. 90, § 2).

d) *Dispensation From the Proper Laws of an Institute*. The general principle is that superiors, clerical and lay, possess only the power of dispensing that is expressly granted them by the constitutions. The doctrine of authors and the practice of the Holy See in approving constitutions exclude the power of dispensing in articles that concern government, organization, formation and religious profession. However, the constitutions may grant authority to dispense from some of these, for example, various reports of superiors and officials, entrance testimonials of proper law, and the manner of beginning the noviceship. The same sources grant to all superiors the right of dispensing in merely disciplinary articles, temporarily, and at least in favor of individuals.

This power is accordingly possessed by all religious superiors, even when it is not expressly granted but not restricted by the constitutions. In general disciplinary articles refer to the order and regularity of common life, the religious exercises, the apostolate and community duties of the religious. A dispensation may be renewed on its expiration. This power extends to all individuals subject to the superior, that is, all attached to or present in the house or province. Many of the merely disciplinary articles that are expressed absolutely are in fact understood as conditional, as demanding permission for their omission rather than a dispensation, e.g., performance of spiritual duties. Permission may therefore be presumed for their omission in circumstances that justify a presumed permission.

The more common practice of constitutions grants the general superior the faculty of dispensing individual religious, provinces, regions, and houses; that of the provincials and other intermediate superiors, e.g., of regions, extends to individuals and houses; but the faculty of local superiors is restricted to individuals. This more common practice may be followed when it is not contrary to the constitutions, since it manifests what is commonly understood to be a superior's power of dispensing.

Some constitutions have demanded that the general superior have the consent or advice of his or her council for a dispensation of a province or house. Some permit the general superior to dispense the entire institute with either the consent or advice of the council or for a definite occasion. A few institutes have imposed the same restrictions on a provincial for the dispensation of a house or of the province. Some constitutions have granted a local superior the faculty of dispensing the entire community in an urgent case or for a single occasion and grave reason. The constitutions have not mentioned the power of the director of novices to dispense. Since he or she can be said to be the superior of the novices and of the novitiate part of the house, he has the same power of dispensing the novices as a local superior for the community, exclusive of the matters that appertain to the government of the house.

e) *Dispensation in Special or Particular Cases.* When the constitutions empower a superior to dispense in special or particular cases, the faculty extends not only to individuals but also to houses, regions, provinces, and the entire institute, according to the level of the superior, provided the reason for the dispensation is sufficiently general, even though not verified in everyone, and the dispensation is granted only temporarily. The reason is sufficiently general when it would be difficult or inopportune to restrict it to those in whom the reason is actually verified. A superior whose power of dispensing is limited to individuals may by the one act dispense all individuals of a community if he or she knows that the reason for the dispensation is verified in all these individuals. He is then dispensing the individuals, not the community, as such.

f) *Dispensation of Oneself.* Any religious superior may directly dispense himself in matters in which he is competent to dispense others, even if such a power is not expressly stated but not denied in the constitutions.

g) *Dispensation From the Laws of the Church.* A dispensation or permission regarding a canonical or common law or decree of the Holy See of itself demands recourse to the Holy See and usually, for consecrated institutes, specifically to the SCRSI, unless the faculty to give the dispensation or permission has been granted to higher superiors, local ordinaries or the apostolic delegate or nuncio. The latest listing of the faculties of the local ordinaries and the apostolic delegate can be found in O'Connor, *Canon Law Digest*, (eight volumes and annual supplements).

h) *Obligation of the Rule and Constitutions.* These, especially the constitutions, are composed of several species of laws.

(1) *Laws of God.* These, e.g., the prohibition of stealing or of lying, whether the law is natural or revealed, oblige immediately under sin, mortal or venial, according to the particular law. Such laws are rarely found in constitutions.

(2) *Laws That Determine the Matter of the Sacred Bonds.* These are also few in number, since they are ordinarily confined to the articles that give the definitions of each bond. Such laws evidently oblige in the same way as the sacred bond because they define the matter of the particular bond. A particular article may also contain a precept in virtue of the vow or other bond of obedience. Such articles are almost never found in the constitutions of lay institutes.

(3) *Laws of the Church.* A number of these, especially those apply-

ing to the consecrated life, are found in all constitutions. They oblige immediately under sin, mortal or venial, according to the law. However, practically none of these laws are encountered in the individual daily life of members of the consecrated states.

(4) *Proper Laws of the Institute*. These are divided into exhortations or counsels, legal, merely disciplinary, and spiritual articles.

a) *Exhortations or Counsels*. It is not repugnant that some articles of the constitutions be merely exhortations or counsels, such as those on the practice of virtue to an exalted degree, e.g., charity, humility, obedience, mortification, and so forth. Of this nature are articles that demand a perfect love of God and complete detachment from self-love in all actions, the acceptance and desire of only what our Lord accepted and desired, complete conformity of judgment in all obedience. If understood in the particular institute as *counsels*, they produce no obligation; if understood as *preceptive*, they are violated only by a habitual neglect to cultivate such virtues.

b) *Legal Articles*. Some of these are on government and organization, e.g., the following matters established by the law of the constitutions: the system of electing delegates to the provincial and general chapters, the number required for a valid session of a chapter or council, the qualities required for various offices, the term of office and immediate reelection or reappointment of superiors and officials, matters that require the vote of a council, the higher superiors competent for admission to the noviceship and the professions, and a temporary profession longer than three years.

c) *Merely Disciplinary Articles*. In general such articles refer to the order and regularity of community life, the religious exercises, the work, when, how and where to make the annual retreat, daily Mass, recitation of the Liturgy of the Hours, silence, mental prayer, prescribed visits to the Blessed Sacrament and monthly recollection, etc.

d) *Spiritual Articles*. These enjoin the practice of various virtues and principles of the spiritual life.

Obligation. Authors usually have treated this matter under the heading of the obligation of the rule, but they understand rule here to include not only Rule properly so called, e.g., that of St. Augustine, but also the constitutions. Quite commonly they included also the legitimate customs, ordinances of the general and provincial chapters, if the latter had such authority and the regulations of superiors. We are following the same complete sense.

The question of the obligation of the proper law of an institute is confined to the articles described in nos. (4) (b), (c) and (d) because the obligation of other articles was stated in defining them. Constitutions have the moral obligation that the legislator imposed. This can be immediately under sin, as may be true of some prescripts of more ancient religious institutes. In several older institutes and later institutes in general, the obligation of the constitutions is stated: they do not of themselves bind directly or immediately under sin. Some add the phrase: but under the penalty imposed for their violation.

All authors admit that the constitutions effect a real obligation. No Rule or constitutions consist entirely of counsels or exhortations. The essential effect of law is to produce an obligation. Some ancient and modern authors have denied that the Rule and constitutions are laws, but this does not imply that they deny also an obligation to observe the Rule and constitutions.

That which is commanded or forbidden by the articles of such constitutions is not enjoined immediately under sin, e.g., the violation of silence is not in itself a sin. There is no dispute on this point because these constitutions expressly exclude such an obligation. The legislator of these laws or statutes is not indifferent to the observation of his laws. He wills the observance of the law. An obligation immediately under sin is not necessary to secure the observance of the constitutions from members of the consecrated life, and a legislator should not impose an obligation greater than is necessary for observance and the common good.

Members of the consecrated life are certainly more prone to observance than to violation of law. Another way of stating the same argument is that sins are not to be multiplied without necessity. An obligation under sin would also cause unnecessary anxieties of conscience. Since profession is a free and spontaneous consecration of oneself to Christ, it is becoming also that the living of this consecration should not be lacking in these same qualities of freedom, spontaneity and generosity. A consecrated member who violates his constitutions under the rationalization that they do not oblige under sin overturns the very reasons for which his constitutions exclude such an obligation, as is evident from the reasons listed above. He has a disposition exactly contrary to that presumed by his constitutions. If consecrated members were commonly of this disposition, the only reasonable norm of a legislator would be to make the constitutions oblige immediately under sin.

All authors admit that the violation of such constitutions is in itself a positive imperfection. This is defined as the omission of a good that is not commanded under sin but in the concrete circumstances is known certainly to be a greater good for the person concerned, either from the clear illumination and inspiration of the Holy Spirit, the certain judgment of reason, or the declaration of legitimate authority given through oral directives or such a medium as constitutions of the consecrated life. A dispute exists among theologians as to whether a positive imperfection is a sin in itself but the more common opinion denies that it is a sin. The effect of such an imperfection is the lessening of worthiness for higher and more efficacious graces from God.

The dispute as to whether a positive imperfection is a sin in itself is of little practical import, since all authors declare, particularly of a violation of constitutions, that such an act is rarely lacking in at least some venial malice either from the effects or the motive of this rejection of a greater good. Sinfulness from the effects is verified when the violation causes scandal, a relaxation of discipline, or other harm. The sinful motive can be anger, impatience, pride, vanity, sloth, sensuality, etc. A religious penitent may therefore accuse himself of violations of the constitutions in confession both for guidance and because these violations rarely lack at least some venial malice.

All theologians and canonists also agree that a subject is obliged under sin to accept and perform a punishment or penance imposed by a superior for a violation of the constitutions. Some hold that this obligation arises wholly or at least partially from the constitutions themselves; others maintain that the obligation has its source purely in the precept of the superior imposing the punishment. There is little practical difference in these two theories. In the latter doctrine, the punishment will not oblige immediately under sin unless it is expressly so imposed by a precept of a superior. However, in practice this is true also in the first opinion. It would be contrary to the spirit of such constitutions if all punishments, even when very slight, were considered as imposed immediately under sin. Therefore, also in the first opinion, the punishment will not oblige immediately under sin unless it is so imposed explicitly or implicitly by the precept of a superior.

> "Therefore, let all members of the states of striving for evangelical perfection remember, and frequently recall before God, that it is not enough for the fulfillment of the obligations of their profession to avoid grave sins, or with the help of God, even venial sins; nor is it enough to carry out only materially the commands of their superiors, or to observe the vows or bonds binding in conscience, or even to observe their own constitutions according to which, as the Church herself commands in the sacred canons, 'each and every religious, superiors as well as subjects, ought . . . to order his life and thus strive for the perfection of his state.' They should accomplish all these things with a wholehearted intention and a burning love, not only out of necessity, 'but also for conscience's sake.' In order to be capable of ascending the summit of sanctity, and of being living founts of Christian charity for all, they must be impelled by the most ardent love for God and their neighbor and adorned with every virtue" (Pius XII, *Sedes Sapientiae*, no. 24).

Violation From Contempt. It is evident that a sin is committed whenever the constitutions are violated from a sinful motive. Formal contempt is the despising of a superior, a law or a counsel as such. It is therefore the contemning or despising of authority. This is a mortal sin, because to despise authority is to despise God, from whom all authority proceeds. Formal contempt is rarely found in the faithful and less frequently in consecrated members. The contempt stated in constitutions is formal contempt. Despite its rare occurrence, constitutions of lay institutes have almost universally mentioned contempt as a sinful motive. It seems to me that it would be more realistic to state that consecrated members sin whenever they violate the constitutions through a sinful motive. This is particularly true of constitutions which word the pertinent article as if contempt were the only sinful motive.

Material contempt is the despisal of the person of a superior or of the matter of a law or counsel, e.g., if a consecrated member despises a legislator as ignorant, imprudent, uncultured, malicious, obstinate, or a law as ridiculous and because of such a motive violates the constitutions. This is ordinarily a venial sin. The sin will be mortal if such a motive leads to a serious violation of the sacred bonds, the serious harm of the institute, grave scandal, or to the proximate occasion of grave sin.

Specific Sinfulness. The sinfulness in a violation is from the subjective motive or the circumstances or both. Therefore the precise sin is that of the motive or circumstances. For example, if such constitutions are violated from pride, the sin is pride; if the circumstances are such as to cause scandal, the sin is against charity. Both malices can be found in the one act. If the constitutions obliged immediately under sin, the primary malice would be from the object, e.g., the violation of such a law of fast would be against the virtue of temperance.

Exemption. Can. 593 declares that all pontifical institutes, clerical and lay, are immediately and exclusively subject to the Apostolic See in their internal government and discipline. Can. 591 leaves the definition and extent of exemption undetermined. Presumably the principle is that exempt institutes and their members are under the authority of the local ordinaries only in the matters in which this subjection is expressly stated in particular canons or in other sources of common law. (A list of the matters of this subjection is found in Vatican II, CD, no. 35; *Ecclesiae sanctae*, ES I, no. 25; and in various numbers of the document, *Mutual Relations between Religious and Bishops*, ND, May 14, 1978.)

a) *Exemption is not Freedom From the Authority of the Holy See.* Can. 488, 2° defined an exempt institute as a "religious institute of either solemn or simple vows that has been withdrawn from the jurisdiction of the local ordinary.'' It is consequently evident that exemption implies no freedom from the authority of the Roman Pontiff or the Roman Congregations.

Canonical authors of the past also gave the purpose of exemption at least principally as the ''preservation and promotion of the unity of a religious institute.'' Some deduced, not with complete logic, the absolute principle that exemption was in possession and to be presumed, exceptions were to be proved. It would have been more logical to have expressed the principle as, ''in possession with regard to the internal life of an institute,'' which is affirmed of all pontifical institutes in the new canon law. The internal life does not extend to the public celebration of the liturgy, clerical deportment and dress, the apostolate and social work for externs, and similar matters. Internal life may be described as the relation of members to the superiors of an institute, the constitutions, directory or statutes, and the proper law in general, as also the charism, spirit, nature, end, character, sound traditions of an institute, and its doctrinal, spiritual and liturgical heritage. Vatican II, *Bishops* (CD), no. 35, 3, defines the purpose of exemption, which is also repeated in other documents:

> ''The privilege of exemption, by which religious are called to the service of the Roman Pontiff or other ecclesiastical authority and are withdrawn from the jurisdiction of bishops, applies chiefly to the internal order of their communities so that in them all things may be more aptly coordinated and the growth and depth of religious life better served. These communities are also exempt in order that the Supreme Pontiff may make use of them for the good of the universal Church or that any other competent authority may do so for the good of the churches under its own jurisdiction.''

John Paul II. The pope has more than once expressed the following principle absolutely, ''religious, like all the faithful, are placed under the jurisdiction of the bishops for the works of the apostolate.''

Ecclesiae sanctae, I, no. 29, includes also the following practical distinction and norms:

"29, § 1. Works proper or peculiar to the Institute, which are carried on in its own houses, even if these are rented, depend on the Superiors of the Institute, who regulate and direct them according to the Constitutions. However, these works also are subject to the jurisdiction of the local Ordinary according to law.

"§ 2. Works which have been entrusted to the Institute by the local Ordinary, however, even though they may be proper or peculiar to it, are under the authority and direction of the same Ordinary, but without prejudice to the right of religious Superiors to exercise vigilance over the life of the members of the Institute and, cumulatively with the local Ordinary, over the fulfillment of the work entrusted to them."

b) *Practical Fields in Which Exempt Religious are Subject to the Local Ordinary*
(1) Vatican II, Bishops (CD)
1. Insofar as, according to law, the performance of the local ordinary's pastoral office and the right ordering of the care of souls requires subjection (no. 35, 4)
2. The care of souls (*ibid.*)
3. Sacred preaching intended for the people (*ibid.*)
4. The public exercise of divine worship, that is in churches, public oratories, and semipublic oratories which in fact are habitually open to the faithful, or if the faithful ordinarily have access to them (*ibid.*). The local ordinary can conduct a visitation of such places concerning the observance of the general law and of episcopal decrees on divine worship. If he discovers any abuse in this matter, after he has notified the superior to no avail, he can take appropriate action on his own authority (ES, no. 38)
5. The religious and moral education of the faithful, especially of children, catechetical instruction, and liturgical formation (*ibid.*)
6. Proper clerical decorum
7. In the various works which concern the exercise of the sacred apostolate (*ibid.*)
8. Catholic schools as regards general policy and supervision (*ibid.*)

9. All things legitimately prescribed by episcopal councils or conferences for universal observance (*ibid.*)

(2) *Motu proprio, Ecclesiae sanctae*, August 6, 1966, O'Connor, *Canon Law Digest*, vol. 6, pp. 264-98 (ES)

10. Matters that concern the sacred apostolate and social action which is prescribed or recommended by the local ordinary (no. 25)

11. Public use of all means of social communication according to nos. 20 and 21 of the Vatican II *Decree on the Means of Social Communication* (*ibid.*)

12. Attendance at public shows (*ibid.*)

13. Enrollment in or cooperation with societies or associations which the local ordinary or the episcopal conference has agreed should be avoided (*ibid.*)

14. Ecclesiastical attire . . . and according to the following stipulation: the local ordinary or the conference of bishops, to avoid astonishment among the faithful, can forbid clerics, whether secular or religious, even the exempt, to wear lay dress in public (*ibid.*)

15. Regulations by the episcopal conference on the seeking of alms (no. 27)

16. Religious should not collect funds by public subscription without the consent of the ordinaries of the places of collection (*ibid.*)

(3) *Mutual Relations between Bishops and Religious*, May 14, 1978, of the two Sacred Congregations for Bishops and for Religious and Secular Institutes (ND)

17. "Even when there is question of documents and other publications issued by local or national religious institutions which, though not meant for the general public, can have a certain influence in pastoral matters (for example, that are in any way connected with faith and religious life), an understanding with the competent ordinaries is necessary and is always to be maintained" (no. 33, b) (see RfR, 41 [1981], pp. 780-2). See can. 591.

592, § 1. *Report to the Holy See*. The general superior, in the manner and at the times stipulated by the Apostolic See, is to send to the latter a brief report on the state and life of the institutes. Possibly the headings of the report will be published later in an instruction from the Holy See. The general superior has been commonly understood as the general superior in a pontifical or diocesan centralized institute. Nothing is therefore said in the canon on the obligation of federations, confederations, and autonomous monasteries and houses to make a report to the Apostolic See.

§ 2. *Documents of the Holy See.* The superiors, especially the major superiors, of all institutes of the consecrated life should evidently promote the knowledge and observance of the documents of the Holy See that concern the members entrusted to them. The necessity of such knowledge and promotion by superiors is most evident.

596, § 1. *Authority.* All superiors possess authority over the members according to universal law and the constitutions. No name is given to this authority, as in the former can. 501, § 1, where it was called "dominative power." This authority is given only to superiors and chapters, not to the members in general of houses, provinces or institutes. Therefore, the SCRSI has frequently insisted that there must be individual general, provincial and local superiors with personal authority. The determined authority that each superior possesses is learned from the provisions of universal law and the constitutions. Usually the authority is at least in general evident from the name, e.g., that of the general superior, who necessarily has authority over the entire institute, and all provinces, houses and members. The authority to govern also extends to the administration of temporal goods (636, § 1).

By incorporation into the institute, the members become subject to the laws and the superiors of the institute. The provincial and local superiors must possess the authority necessary at least for the normal government of the province and the houses on the provincial, or intermediate, and local levels. This authority extends to giving a precept under sin and to a member as a subject, apart from the special bond, although in fact such a precept would frequently be given in virtue of the special bond of obedience. This authority implies an imperfect judicial power, e.g., whether or not the constitutions were violated, and a coercive power of imposing the penances in use in the particular institute. According to § 3 of the present canon, the norms of can. 131, 133 and 137-144 apply also to the authority of can. 596, § 1. The more practical of these norms are on the distinction of ordinary and delegated power and the supplying of power in common error and in a positive and probable doubt.

§ 2. In pontifical clerical religious institutes, superiors, and chapters possess also, according to the norms of the constitutions, the ecclesiastical power of governing, or jurisdiction, for the external and internal forum. In virtue of this power, the general chapter may make laws in such institutes. In fact the government of these institutes also is normally by the common authority of paragraph one, since the ecclesiastical power is employed usually only in such matters as making laws and the confessions of the members.

597. This canon will be explained later under "admission to a religious institute."

598, § 1. *Evangelical Counsels in General*. Can. 598-601 treat of the evangelical counsels as found in all institutes of consecrated life, whether they are religious or secular institutes. Since the purpose of these counsels is often omitted or stated incompletely, inaccurately or obscurely, I believe it is necessary to give first the proof that the immediate purpose of the evangelical counsels is negative.

The goal of every member is to strive for sanctity of life, which consists principally in acts of the infused and supernatural virtue of charity. "Charity is a theological virtue infused by God into the will by which we love God above all things for himself and ourselves and the neighbor for love of God" (Royo Marin, *Teologia della perfezione cristiana*, no. 254). Sanctity of life evidently includes all virtues, but charity is the principal virtue, both in itself and as the motivating force of all other virtues. This charity is not to be lived in an abstract manner but in the personal manner of loving and living Christ. It can therefore be said that a member primarily professes charity and professes chastity, poverty and obedience as means to charity.

The counsels are negative means to the great positive of charity because they control the principal obstacles to charity: chastity, the divided heart; poverty, the fascination of material things; obedience, the excessive love of self, or pride. The first proof of this negative purpose is in the official definitions of the public vows of the counsels, which are all negative, namely, by chastity one gives up marriage and external and interior acts against chastity; by poverty, he renounces the proprietary disposition of material things; and obedience is the renunciation of one's own will in so many aspects of life. Theological proofs are certainly not lacking for this doctrinal position. The immediately negative purpose is clearly affirmed in Vatican II.

> "However, in order that he may be capable of deriving more abundant fruit from this baptismal grace, he intends by the profession of the evangelical counsels in the Church, to free himself from such obstacles which might draw him away from the fervor of charity" (*liberari intendit ab impedimentis, quae ipsum a caritatis fervore . . . retrahere possent. . . .*) (LG, n. 44). "For the counsels, voluntarily undertaken according to each one's personal vocation, contribute greatly to purification of heart and spiritual liberty" (*ad cordis purificationem et spiritualem libertatem non parum conferunt*) (*ibid.*, no. 46). ". . . it [chastity] frees the heart of man in a unique fashion (see 1 Cor. 7:32-5) so that it may be more inflamed with love for God and for all men" (PC, n. 12).

Modern popes have taught the immediate negative purpose.

> "Everyone who commits himself, by a solemn undertaking made to God, to observe these counsels, is freed from the hindrances which impede mortal men on the way to sanctity . . ." (Pius XI, *Apostolic Letter on the Studies of Religious*, Courtois, *The States of Perfection*, n. 130). "But your special role is to make use of the most efficient means, namely the evangelical counsels by the taking of the vows of religion; thus by assiduous warfare you will vanquish the concupiscence of the flesh; the concupiscence of the eyes and the pride of life . . ." (Pius XII, *Allocution to the International Congress of Religious*, December 8, 1950, Courtois, *ibid.*, n. 421). ". . . on the other hand, the mind of one who is burdened by

the cares and ties of matrimony is always to some extent divided''
(Pius XII, *Encyclical on Christian Virginity*, March 25, 1954,
Courtois, *ibid.*, n. 504).
The negative purpose was more precisely expressed in a letter of the
Papal Secretary of State, July 13, 1952: "The state of perfection is so
called and is such, inasmuch as, through the medium of the three
evangelical counsels, it removes the principal obstacles which impede
the effort to obtain personal sanctity; or, to speak more exactly, it is by its
nature suited to the removal of these obstacles" (Courtois, *ibid.*, n. 474).

St. Thomas also held the negative purpose. "Secondarily and instru-
mentally, however, perfection consists in the observance of the
counsels, all of which, like the commandments, are directed to
charity . . . whereas the counsels are directed to the removal of things
that hinder the act of charity, and yet are not contrary to charity, such as
marriage, the occupation of worldly business, and so forth" (*ST* II, II, q.
184, a. 3, 3). This negative purpose has been affirmed by many authors,
especially those who follow St. Thomas. ". . . the counsels are limited to
removing the obstacles that impede the facile and prompt exercise of
charity. It seems clear, therefore, that the counsels are not essential for
Christian perfection but only a very useful instrument to better attain it"
(Royo Marin, *Teologia della perfezione cristiana*, n. 117).

"Besides this fidelity [to the religious vows] renders singularly easy
the exercise of the love of God by detaching the soul from the chief
obstacles which stand in the way of divine charity. *Poverty*, by uprooting
disordered love for wealth, sets the heart free to reach out to God and
heavenly things. *Chastity*, by spurning the pleasures of the flesh, even
those the holy state of marriage would sanction, fosters an undivided
love of God. *Obedience*, by fighting pride and the spirit of independence, subjects the will to that of God. This obedience is, in reality, a
genuine act of love" (Tanquerey, *The Spiritual Life*, n. 338). "But
because the Evangelical Counsels remove the greatest impediments to
the full dominion of charity over man's life, namely the love of riches,
the pleasures of the flesh, honors and independence, it follows that the

observance of these opposing counsels of poverty, perfect continence and voluntary obedience makes striving after perfection easier, safer, and more efficacious'' (de Guibert, *The Theology of the Spiritual Life*, n. 84).

The present canon affirms that every institute should define in its constitutions, in accord with its distinctive end, character, and manner of life, the way in which the evangelical counsels of chastity, poverty and obedience must be observed. The religious profession of the counsels will be given in full later.

§ 2. *Manner of Striving for Perfection.* This is can. 593 of the 1917 code. It says that all members must observe the counsels and also their own proper law, both of which are evident, and continues, '' . . . and thus strive for the perfection of their state.'' I think the sense is, "and thus living Christ more completely strive for the perfection of their state.'' This is based on the principle that the Christ of the gospel is the supreme rule and also on the necessity of excluding the danger of having consecrated life understood as the observance of law for itself.

Obligation of Striving for Perfection. Perfection here is sanctity of life, which consists principally in the perfection of charity. All authors admit an obligation to strive for perfection but they differ in explaining its source.

The first and solidly probable opinion is that this obligation is completely identified with the obligation of observing the evangelical counsels and the proper law of the institute. The arguments for this opinion are (1) canon law does not assert a distinct obligation of striving for perfection; (2) can. 598, § 2 appears to identify the obligation of striving for perfection with that of observing the evangelical counsels and the constitutions; (3) one who fulfills the duties of a state of life fulfills its end; (4) one obliged to the means of perfection is sufficiently bound to strive for perfection itself; (5) all are obliged to strive for eternal salvation but not by an obligation distinct from obeying the laws and other obligations to which one is subject. The second opinion asserts a distinct obligation to strive for perfection because (1) a member is obliged to strive for the purpose of his state of life; (2) from the tacit promise in profession to strive for the purpose of his state; and (3) one who promises a definite means to an end also promises to strive for the end. All these may be true but they do not certainly require a distinct obligation to strive for perfection. They are satisfied sufficiently by the obligation to observe the distinctive means, the evangelical counsels and the constitutions.

599. *Definition and Purpose of Consecrated Chastity*. The purpose of chastity is given as the exclusion of the divided heart in order that one may give his total love to God in Christ our Lord. In its object this chastity is twofold, of celibacy and perfect chastity. Celibacy, in its proper sense, is not to marry. Accordingly the obligation forbids marriage directly and in itself, so that contracting or attempting marriage is in itself and directly contrary to consecrated chastity. This obligation is also one of perfect chastity. Its object is that of the virtue, namely, it forbids everything already forbidden to the unmarried by the sixth and ninth commandments. Hence, the professed has a twofold obligation of perfect chastity, from the virtue of chastity by the commandments and from the bond of his institute. Consecrated chastity has the same object therefore in all institutes of consecrated life. The official definition, because it has been followed by the Roman Congregations at least since the Normae of 1901, was as follows, *"By the vow of chastity, religious bind themselves to a life of celibacy and, by a new obligation from the virtue of religion, to abstain from any internal or external act opposed to chastity."*

600. *Definition of the Poverty of the Consecrated Life*.

This definition of poverty in the consecrated life is obscure. The canon states that the counsel of poverty implies "dependence," which has been the only object of the vow in the past, that is, the exclusion of disposing of temporal goods as one's own. The canon adds, "dependence and limitation." Limitation in the past has been the object of law, as in the former can. 594, § 3. The whole canon is affected by the qualification, "according to the norm of proper law." The canon also requires a "life poor in fact" and one "foreign to earthly riches." The profession of poverty has been understood as excluding superfluities, whereas the term used in the canon, "moderation," would permit some super-fluities. "Moderation" may have been chosen with the secular state of members of secular institutes in mind. The official definition of the religious vow of poverty has been, *"By the vow of poverty, religious renounce the right of disposing licitly of any temporal thing of monetary value without the permission of their lawful superior."*

601. *Definition of the Counsel of Obedience.* This counsel will not vary much in different institutes because it has been essentially an obligation to obey as a religious, in matters appertaining at least indirectly to the religious life. This will undoubtedly be the principle also of secular institutes. They should likewise attend to the conditions required to effect an obligation from the essential bond of obedience, which will be given under "religious obedience."

602. *Common or Community Life.* By the former can. 487 community life was an essential requisite of religious institutes. Common life de-manded that one be a member of a religious institute, approved as such by the Church; that he or she live under a common superior, according to the proper law of the institute; and , more specifically, that his whole social life be with other members of the institute by living under the same roof, eating and recreating together, and so forth. The Holy See, at least by way of dispensation, could and did approve as religious institutes associations that possessed only the first two elements of common life, but such institutes were very few in number. The force of the require-ment of common life was strengthened by the sufficiently stringent limitations on absences of can. 606, § 2.

The present can. 602 enjoins that the common life "proper to each institute" is to be so defined in the proper law that it is a "mutual aid to all for the fulfillment of their proper vocation," that is, in striving for sanctity of life and the accomplishment of the apostolate. The very nature of common life demands also that all the members make it a means of developing their social qualities and of cooperating in making the community life socially satisfactory to all. Finally, the canon de-clares that the community life, rooted in charity, should be an example of the universal reconciliation in Christ. The canon thus states what is very evident in fact: that charity from all members to all members is necessary for the community life intended by the Church.

603. *Eremetical Life.* The canon declares concerning the life of individual hermits: " . . . the Church recognizes the eremetical or anchoretic life, by which faithful of Christ, through a stricter separation from the world, silence of solitude and assiduous prayer and penance, devote their life to the praise of God and the salvation of the world. A hermit is recognized in law by the Church as dedicated to God in the consecrated life, if he publicly professes in the hand of the diocesan bishop the three counsels by vow or other sacred bond and observes his own manner of life under the leadership of the same."

604. *Order of Virgins.* This canon states that the order of virgins is related to the forms of consecrated life and describes this order: "These, emitting the intention of following Christ more closely, according to the approved liturgical rite are consecrated to God by the diocesan bishop, mystically espoused to Christ, the Son of God, and dedicated to the service of the Church. Virgins may form associations for the more faithful observance of their intention and the service of the Church consonant with their state and in order to carry this out with mutual aid."

605. *Approval of New Forms of Consecrated Life.* This approval is reserved exclusively to the Apostolic See. Diocesan bishops must strive to discern new gifts of consecrated life entrusted to the Church by the Holy Spirit. They can be aided by the description and criteria of the charism of founders given above under can. 4-5 from the document of May 14, 1978 on *the Relations between Bishops and Religious.* The present canon also advises the bishops to aid the promoters of new forms of consecrated life to a better expression of their proposals and their safeguarding by appropriate statutes, as likewise to use the general norms of this section for such purposes.

606. *Common Law Applicable Equally to Both Sexes.* Enactments of the new code or of subsequent general legislation concerning members of the consecrated state apply equally to men and women, unless the contrary is clear from the context of the wording or from the nature of the

matter. It is evident for example, that enactments on the reception and exercise of sacred orders and priestly ministries concern only male and clerical members of institutes of consecrated life.

CHAPTER II

RELIGIOUS INSTITUTES

This and the following chapters are all on religious institutes and their members.

607. *Public Vows, Stability and Separation From the World*. Most of what is said in this entire canon is merely another way of expressing what was already affirmed in can. 573 and 602.

a) *Public Vows*. In the first schema only the perpetual religious profession had to be by public vow. The temporary profession could be by public vow or some other bond, e.g., an oath, promise, consecration or private vow. In the revised version both perpetual and temporary religious professions must be by public vows. In secular institutes and societies of apostolic life, the bond is one different from public vows, as those listed above (can. 573, § 2). Can. 1192, § 1 retains the same definition of a public vow as in the past: "A vow is public if accepted in the name of the Church by a legitimate superior; otherwise it is private."

b) *Stability*. Can. 573, § 1 had demanded stability in all institutes of consecrated life. The present can. 607, § 2 states of temporary vows, as in the past, that they are to be renewed on their expiration. The religious life has always demanded stability and still does so. From its concept it is a state of life in the same way as the clerical or married state. A state of life contains the propriety of stability or permanence. The exact permanence required is defined by the Church as follows: perpetual vows are sufficient but not necessary; the minimum requisite is temporary vows. Therefore, an institute in which all the members make only annual professions of chastity, poverty and obedience fulfills this requisite. In fact institutes of only temporary vows are most rarely found. The Church further requires that temporary vows are to be renewed on their expiration. This clause obtains the permanence that is not found in the temporary vows considered only in themselves. The sense of the clause is:

1) A religious is not obliged to renew the vows on their expiration because any religious may freely leave an institute on the expiration of the vows.

2) The clause excludes from the religious state an institute that would have only temporary vows and not permit the renewal of these vows.

3) The clause implies an intention on the part of both the one making temporary profession and the superior admitting to this profession that, if no obstacle arises in the meantime, the vows will be renewed on their expiration.

4) However, if the one making the temporary profession or the superior admitting to it had the intention, even externally manifested, of not renewing or not admitting to a further profession, the profession would be illicit but not invalid because the canons nowhere expressly invalidate such a profession.

c) *Separation From the World.* The third paragraph of this canon states, ''The public testimony to be given to the Church and Christ by religious implies that separation from the world proper to each institute.'' Can. 602 had demanded, certainly in religious institutes, that there be a community life proper to each institute. Such a separation is also implicitly enacted by can. 608: ''A religious community must reside in a house legitimately constituted under the authority of a superior designated in accordance with the norm of law. The individual houses shall have at least an oratory in which the Eucharist is celebrated and reserved so that it is truly the center of the community.'' Evidently the separation should be greater for the purely contemplative than for the immediately and directly apostolic religious. Separation also arises from cloister. Certainly, a reasonable privacy of life is to be guaranteed to all religious, and an ''open house'' policy permitting the entrance of seculars to any part of the house and almost at any hour is contrary to the separation from the world and the religious atmosphere that should characterize any religious house. Under can. 667, § 1 we find the prescript, "A part of the religious house shall always be reserved to the members alone."

Religious Houses

608. *Residence of Religious*. The canon commands a religious community to reside, under the authority of a superior designated according to law, in a legitimately constituted house. The individual houses shall have at least an oratory (the former semipublic oratory) in which the Eucharist is celebrated and reserved so that it is truly the center of the community. "By the term *church* is understood a sacred building destined for divine worship to which the faithful have the right to go to exercise divine worship especially publicly" (can. 1214). "By the term *oratory* is understood a place designated with the permission of the ordinary for divine worship for the advantage of some community or assembly of the faithful who gather there. Other members of the faithful can also have access to it with the consent of the competent superior" (can. 1223). "By the term *private chapel* is understood a place designated for divine worship for the advantage of one or many physical persons, with the permission of the local ordinary" (can. 1226).

609. *Canonical Erection of Religious Houses*. The following distinct meanings of *house* are to be kept in mind.

Secular House. The stable residence of its members and the customary tenor of life of the institute are necessary to have a religious house. Therefore a mere summer residence owned, rented or granted temporarily to an institute and used only as a summer vacation place, is not a religious but a secular house. No permission of the diocesan bishop is necessary to build or open such a summer or similar residence. It would frequently be a duty of courtesy to consult him previously.

Material Sense of a House. This is the house or building in which the members reside; but all buildings located within the same property, grounds or premises, and buildings not separated from that in which the members reside are considered part of the religious house, e.g., separate buildings on the same grounds for a college, a preparatory school, an elementary school, library, science building, infirmary, field house, and houses for workmen and their families are all part of the religious house. Even when not on the same grounds nor contiguous to the residence of the members, a building is not considered separate if it can be judged to form part of the same group of buildings. It is certainly separate if a mile distant; but a building a few doors away from the residence of the members, even if a street is between them, may still be said to be part of the same group of buildings.

Formal Sense of a House. This is the more important sense of the term and is the same thing as a canonically erected house. It is the community as a distinct juridical person, distinguished from both the province and the institute, which are also juridical persons. It is a subject of rights and obligations, which are distinct from those of its members considered individually or collectively. A juridical person can acquire, own and administer property, is responsible for its debts and obligations, and can sue or be sued in court.

The antecedent requisites for a canonically erected house are: a) at the time of the erection it must consist of at least three members; b) it must be a distinct community with its own proper superior; c) it must be the stable dwelling of the members in the house; and d) in it there should be the customary tenor of life according to its proper constitutions. It is not necessary that an institute be the proprietor of a canonically erected house, a filial house, or a separated establishment. All of these may be owned or rented or their use granted gratuitously to the institute. All may be an entire building or a part of a building, e.g., a floor or an apartment.

Strictly Filial Houses. In some institutes all houses except the motherhouse are called missions, branch houses, or filial houses, which is not the strict sense. The essential character of a *filial house* in the strict sense is that it is not a distinct juridical person but part of the larger canonically erected house to which it is attached. Therefore, the one at the head of a filial house is not a superior in the proper sense of the word, even though he may have this title. He is a mere delegate of a higher superior or of the superior of the canonically erected house to which the filial house is attached, and his authority is as wide as the delegation. He is appointed by a major superior for a specified term, e.g., three years, or for no determined period of time.

Since it is not a juridical person, the filial house does not own property, all of which is owned by the house to which it is attached. Its local treasurer is that of the latter house but he may have an assistant in the filial house. The same principle is true of councilors but there may be equivalent advisers in a filial house. Unless otherwise specified in the constitutions or other proper law, the capitular rights of those residing in the filial house are exercised in the larger house. The number of religious resident in a filial house is usually small. The larger house to which the filial house is attached is ordinarily located in the same city or in a nearby place. Constitutions rarely mention filial houses. All institutes may open filial houses unless this is expressly forbidden by the constitutions.

Civil Incorporation. An institution such as a college conducted by religious is part of the same one juridical person as the religious community, unless the college has been erected into a distinct juridical person through ecclesiastical authority. The latter has been rather unusual in practice. At the very least, the college is owned by an ecclesiastical juridical person, the religious house, and is consequently ecclesiastical or church property. The oneness of juridical personality of the house and its work has been evident in canon law. For example, a change in the external work of a religious house, such as changing a hospital into a home for the aging, required, by the former can. 497, § 2, a new erection of the religious community as a juridical person. The juridical persons of a religious institute were also constantly listed as the institute, provinces, and houses.

This oneness of juridical personality is not changed by mere separate civil incorporation of the college. Religious in fact have lost general control of their colleges by such an incorporation. They have also lost the effective administration of their temporal property, which is alienation. Obviously the motive of such an incorporation should never be to remove an institution from subjection to legitimate Church authority. Evidently also, the Holy See, in the past and now, insists that Catholic colleges be truly and in fact Catholic. Clearly, likewise, a Catholic college may not on its own authority become neutral, non-sectarian, not Catholic (see RfR, 27 [1968], 553-61; Maida, *Ownership, Control and Sponsorship of Catholic Institutions*, Harrisburg: Pennsylvania Catholic Conference, 1975).

Local Houses and Juridical Personality. A juridical person in the Church is of its nature perpetual. If only one member remains, all rights of the juridical person devolve on him. A juridical person and therefore one of the religious life becomes extinct only when it has ceased to exist for a hundred years. As a collegial juridical person, a canonically erected house must consist of at least three members at the time of its erection. Since a juridical person is of its nature perpetual, it is evident that the continued existence of a canonically erected house does not depend on the permanent residence of the religious who originally constituted the community. These may constantly change as they do in other juridical persons, e.g., an institute or a province.

The same juridical perpetuity proves that a canonically erected house continues to exist as such if the number of religious after its erection becomes less than three. The superior of such a reduced house remains a superior in the proper sense of the word, since he is the superior of a canonically erected house. A major superior cannot change a canonically erected house into a filial house merely by assigning less religious to it. This change demands an extinction or the formalities of a suppression and the opening of a filial house. Neither may he change a filial house into a canonically erected house merely by assigning more religious to it. This change requires the formalities of a canonical erection.

Essential Canonical Requirements. The canon requires the written consent of the bishop of the location for the canonical erection of a religious house. The erection of a monastery of nuns demands also the permission of the Holy See. The consent of the bishop should also be secured for the establishment of a filial house or the opening of an establishment separated from the canonically erected house, e.g., any type or part of a school, lodging places, homes for the aging, places for the education of candidates, and similar establishments. Such places are separated from, but still part of, the canonically erected house to which they are attached.

If they are not separated but located, at least morally speaking, on the same grounds, no permission of the diocesan bishop is necessary, unless such a work was excluded in the consent for the canonically erected house. This right of the diocesan bishop flows from the facts that the works of the apostolate are in general subject to him and that he is to protect other Catholic institutions, and is aimed at leaving him an unimpeded right of giving or refusing consent to a future canonically erected house at the same location.

Competent Authority of the Institute. Ordinarily the constitutions will prescribe that the general superior canonically erect the house with the consent of his council in a centralized institute, preceded by the favorable act of the provincial superior with the consent of his council. It would not be contrary to can. 609, § 1 for the erecting authority to be given to provincials, but, in my opinion, at least the confirming act of the general superior should also be demanded. The consent of the councils should be required in all these cases because of the importance of the act. The same necessity of consent of councils should be observed for filial houses and separated establishments. In autonomous monastery or house structures, the consent will commonly at least be that of the chapter. Since can. 609, § 1 explicitly affirms that the competent superior erects the house, it would be better, although not of obligation, that this superior issue a formal decree of erection, a copy of which is to be retained in the house itself and in that of the competent superior.

610. *Antecedent Canonical Requirements.* The conditions stated in this paragraph should be observed also in the opening of a filial house or separated establishment. The canon requires that the erection be made with the utility of the Church and the institute in mind; that all things necessary for the proper living of the religious life by the members be assured, according to the special purposes and spirit of the institute; and that it can be prudently foreseen that the community will have proper living quarters, sustenance and suitable means of support from regular

and dependable sources of income. As far as possible, this should be from its work.

Care must be taken by lay institutes regarding the availability of priests for Mass, confessions, and so forth.

Prudence, equity and charity demand that the diocesan bishop and the competent superiors consider the effect of the proposed erection on the houses of other institutes located in the same territory. This is a matter of a prudent judgment to be based upon a consideration of the good to be attained by the new house and the loss that will be suffered by houses already existing in the locality.

611. *Effects of an Erection.* The consent of the diocesan bishop for the erection of a religious house implies the right:

1) to live a life according to the character, specific ends, and means proper to the institute. This same right had already been given to an institute in a more basic way by its legitimate erection and the approval of its constitutions.

2) to exercise in the house all the works proper to the particular institute, unless some of these were explicitly or implicitly excluded by conditions attached to the consent itself. Therefore, an apostolic institute of Sisters, that includes in its purpose the teaching of youth, nursing, and homes for the orphaned and aged, may exercise all these works in a house that has been legitimately erected. A just reason for imposing limitations is the desire of the diocesan bishop to provide for the needs of his diocese in a fair and equitable manner and to avoid harmful competition and rivalry among religious institutes or between them and the diocesan priests.

The canon requires that the restrictions be attached to the consent. The restrictions of the diocesan bishop will frequently be implicit, e.g., that he consented to the erection of a house to conduct a school, not for other major works with no relation to the school. A consent could have been given years ago for a general motherhouse, which certainly extended to buildings for the general superior and officials, a postulancy, novitiate, juniorate and central infirmary.

May this institute, without any added consent of the diocesan bishop, now establish a nursing home for externs on the same grounds? There may be two other nursing homes of other religious institutes already existing nearby for many years. If no consent of the diocesan bishop is required, it is difficult to see the application of the admitted principle that works of the apostolate are under the diocesan bishop. How could he otherwise provide fairly for all institutes and how could he be held to foresee all possible works that religious institutes may later wish to establish? It seems to me that the interpretation of the canon should exclude, without the added consent of the diocesan bishop, the later inception of major works that do not reasonably flow from the original consent for the religious house.

3) For clerical institutes to have a church, i.e., church or public oratory as understood in the past, but to locate the church in a certain and determined place, another permission of the diocesan bishop is necessary by can. 1215, § 3.

Sacred Ministry. Any clerical institute is given also the right of exercising the sacred ministry, e.g., to say Mass, preach and hear confessions. However the institute is obviously to observe here the dependence on the local ordinary demanded by canon law in particular matters, by securing from him the faculty to preach, hear confessions, and so forth.

612. *Mere Material Change of a House.* This is a change that in no way alters the purpose of the house, e.g., renovating, repairing, enlarging, or rebuilding the house, and the construction or addition of other buildings, e.g., a library, classroom building, auditorium, infirmary, and so forth. Such a change demands no permission of any Church authority outside the institute.

Formal but Merely Internal Change. This is a change that affects the state and juridical condition of the house but only within the institute, e.g., the changing of a novitiate into a house of studies, the making of an ordinary house the residence of a provincial. Such a change requires no permission of external authority. A formal internal change may not, however, be made without the consent of the diocesan bishop if it is contrary to a condition he placed at the erection of the house.

Formal External Change. This is a change in the purpose of a house with regard to its apostolic activities on behalf of externs, e.g., of a school into a hospital, of a hospital into a home for the aging, and so forth. Such a change requires the consent of the diocesan bishop. His consent is also necessary for the same change in a filial house or separated establishment. This same principle applies when the change is only partially or secondarily external.

No material or formal change may be made contrary to the terms specified in the foundation of a house, whether this rose from a simple gift or the bequest of a will.

Oratories. The erection of a church requires the written consent of the diocesan bishop. The permission of the ordinary is necessary for an oratory (cc. 1215, § 1; 1223). According to can. 934, § 1, 1°, the Blessed Sacrament should be reserved in "a church or oratory connected with the house of a religious institute." The permission of the ordinary is necessary for a reservation also in another oratory of the same house (can. 936).

613. *Monastic Structure of Monks and Canons Regular.* The canon states that a monastery of monks or canons regular is in itself autonomous, "unless the constitutions state the contrary." This exceptive clause is declaring that a centralized structure may be found among monks and canons regular. Such a structure now exists among contemplative religious women, even if not in great number. It may also express the possibility of derogations from the autonomy of the individual monasteries, which is also something that is always within the authority of the Holy See.

There is in general greater familiarity with the centralized structure. If we begin with the lowest element, such institutes consist of *canonically erected religious houses*, but there can also be separated establishments and filial houses, which are not distinct juridical entities in themselves but part of the house (province or institute), to which they are attached; *provinces* are on the second level. They arise because of such reasons as the size and the extent of the institute and consist of many distinct houses; and, finally, there is the *institute*, which embraces all provinces, houses and members.

There is a parallel distinction of authority: a local superior, who governs a house and its members but only on the local level, e.g., he does not admit to professions nor transfer nor dismiss members; secondly, there is a provincial superior, who is a major superior and governs on the provincial or intermediate level all the houses and members of the province; and lastly, there is a general superior, who governs on the supreme or institute level all members, houses and provinces.

The same distinction is true of the two collegial bodies: 1) *the province chapter*, which elects delegates to the general chapter, elects the provincial and/or the provincial officials in some institutes (and in some institutes also makes enactments for the province, which, in the past practice, had to be confirmed by the general superior with the consent of his council) and makes proposals to the general chapter; 2) *the general chapter*, which elects the general superior and the elective general officials, and makes enactments for the entire institute. The general chapter and the general superior have been put on the same level of supreme authority in the constitutions. Ultimately the superior authority is that of the general chapter because the general superior is also subject to its enactments.

Instead of this double level of house and institute, (or triple level if there are provinces), an autonomous house is essentially a one-house structure, although here also filial houses are possible. There is a superior, who is local in the sense that he or she governs one house and its members. His authority therefore includes the local level but also extends to the level of a major or higher superior, as he is classed by § 2. He does such things as admissions to professions, which does not appertain to a purely local superior. He has a council, as do the superiors in a centralized institute, but there is also a monastery chapter which, unlike the general or provincial chapter of a centralized institute, is also a permanent advisory body.

This is why we find some canons of the 1917 code that state a particular action appertains to a major superior "with the vote of the council or chapter." A general or provincial chapter is an extraordinary matter, a monastery chapter an ordinary one. A monastery chapter acts in an advisory capacity (with the consent or advice of the chapter), not in a purely collegial manner, in which the authority and acts are of the body as such, unless the latter is evident from the nature of the matter or from an express provision of common or proper law. The latter two sources also determine the matters that appertain to the chapter and the council.

614. *Monastery of Nuns Associated with an Institute of Men.* In the past there were nuns, such as the Visitandines, not subject to a religious order of men. Many other nuns, e.g., the Discalced Carmelites, were so subject by their own law, even though in several places and for various historical reasons, this subjection had not existed in fact in many monasteries and for a long time. Can. 614 was no. 106 of the original published schema. It makes two assertions. The first is that the manner of life and government of a monastery associated with an institute of men is determined by the nuns' constitutions. The canon asserts secondly that the mutual rights and obligations are to be so defined that the association is a source of spiritual good.

615. *Autonomous Monastery of Nuns Entrusted to the Special Vigilance of the Diocesan Bishop.* An autonomous monastery of nuns that does not have another higher superior over the proper superior of the monastery, and which furthermore is not so associated with an institute of religious men that the latter's superior possesses true authority, determined by the constitutions, over the monastery, is entrusted according to the norm of law to the special vigilance of the diocesan bishop. This canon was included in a supplementary manner in *Communicationes*, 13 (1981), p. 197.

616. *Suppression of a Religious House.* Suppression is the authoritative withdrawal of the character of a juridical person from an institute, province or house or of the approval of a separated establishment or filial house.

§ 1. The first paragraph states that the suppression of a religious house, with the exceptions noted in the three following paragraphs, appertains to the general superior according to the norm of the constitutions, after consulting the diocesan bishop. The constitutions should also demand the consent of the general council and require likewise the act of the provincial superior with the consent of the provincial council. The proper law of an institute shall contain provisions for the disposition of the property of a suppressed house, but the intentions of founders or donors are to be observed and rights legitimately acquired respected.

§ 2. The suppression of the one house of an institute and the disposal of its property appertain to the Holy See.

§ 3. The suppression of an autonomous house described in can. 613 appertains to the general chapter, unless the constitutions establish otherwise.

§ 4. The suppression of an autonomous monastery of nuns appertains to the Apostolic See, and the norms of the constitutions shall be observed in the disposal of its property.

Nothing is said in the canon on consulting the diocesan bishop regarding the suppression of the houses of the last three paragraphs. I presume that this will at least ordinarily be done in fact.

Superiors and Councils

617, 620-22. *Superiors.* A superior in the proper sense of the term is one who governs at least a canonically erected house. He possesses ordinary authority, which is that given by universal and proper law and not merely by the act of another. (The latter is delegated authority). The religious at the head of a filial house may be called a superior, but is not properly such because he possesses only delegated authority.

The power of all religious superiors is limited by the determination of universal and proper law: the matters reserved to higher authorities, for example, the Holy See, diocesan bishops, conferences of bishops, a general, provincial or local chapter, a superior of higher level in the institute; or which require a deliberative or consultative vote of his council. Otherwise he has the right of governing alone.

However, in the spirit of constitutions as approved by the SCRSI, he should consult his council also in other important matters. Every superior also governs only on his level: for example, a minor local superior, as opposed to one who is also a higher superior of an autonomous monastery or house, does not admit to nor dismiss from the institute because these are evidently matters that transcend the local level.

The principle of the new canon 622 remains the same as in the past: "A general superior has power over all provinces, houses and members of an institute, to be exercised according to proper law. Other superiors possess power within the limits of their office." The authority of the general superior, as also of provincials, is immediate and need not necessarily be exercised through provincials and local superiors. The authority of a provincial superior extends to all houses and members of the province. A regional superior, in the practice of the SCRSI, has had only delegated authority.

However, since he governs on the same intermediate level as a provincial, he or she can be and at least sometimes is, given by delegation all the authority that a provincial possesses from law. For the same reason he should be given *ex officio* membership in the general chapter. A minor local superior (that is, of a canonically erected house) is not a mere delegate of a higher superior. His authority is determined by the universal and proper law. His office of its nature demands at least the authority necessary for the usual government of a house and its members.

Since the general superior has the government of the entire institute and all its members, it is evident that all other superiors are subject to his or her direction and correction and that ordinarily he may rescind and annul their acts. He may not deprive a lower superior of a faculty granted the latter by universal or proper law, because a higher superior also is subject to such laws and must obey them. The higher superior may in a particular case forbid the exercise of such a faculty when this is demanded by the common good, religious discipline, or the elimination of an abuse.

All these principles apply also to a provincial with regard to the superiors under him. A superior may delegate authority except in the cases in which common or proper law excludes delegation. The authority of a religious superior is primarily at least personal, not territorial, which is limited to a particular territory.

Higher Superiors. The following is the definition of higher or major superiors in the new canon 620: "Major superiors are those who govern an entire institute or a province or part equal to the latter or an autonomous house and their vicars. To these the abbot primate and the superior of a monastic congregation are to be added, although they do not have all the power given by universal law to major superiors."

In a centralized institute, the higher superiors are the general and provincial superiors and their vicars—while the last mentioned, who are the general and provincial assistants, are actually exercising the power of a vicar, that is, on the death, resignation, removal, absence, sickness or other impediment of the general or provincial superior.

Others who govern a part equal to provinces are those over vice-provinces, quasi-provinces, custodians, commissariats, visitations, regions, missions, districts and vicariates, provided they possess ordinary and not merely delegated authority. The more usual name for such territories, at least in lay institutes in recent times, has been "regions." A local superior in a centralized institute has thus far been classified as a minor local superior.

The abbot primate is the superior of the confederation of Benedictines wearing the black habit. He is abbot of the monastery of San Anselmo, in Rome. He, along with the superior of a monastic congregation, the union of several autonomous monasteries under one and the same superior, is a higher superior, although they do not have all the power given by universal law to major superiors. The one who governs an autonomous monastery, also of nuns, and his or her vicar when actually acting as such, are higher superiors. The same principles are true of an institute of sisters that has the structure of an autonomous monastery of nuns.

In federations and confederations of nuns, the nun president as such does not possess any authority and is not a superior of the monasteries or federations that appertain to the federation or confederation. Federations can also consist of apostolic religious institutes of men and of women. (The authority of superiors was also partially explained under can. 596, § 1).

618-19. *Counsels for Superiors*. These counsels on the duties of superiors are most important but also evident from a mere reading. One of the counsels is to "lead them to the celebration of the sacred liturgy." The daily celebration of Mass is highly important also for the sanctity of life of the religious priest, which at the present time is by no means universally appreciated.

The Sacred Congregation of Catholic Education, in its *Instruction on Liturgical Formation in Seminaries*, no. 26, strongly emphasizes the counsel of the Church on daily celebration by priests: "In view of some modern ideas spread about here and there, seminarians should be warned about how strongly the Church advises priests to celebrate Mass daily, even if they are not bound to do so by a pastoral obligation or even if the faithful cannot be present. The celebration of the eucharistic sacrifice even then is an action of Christ and the Church offered to God for the salvation of the whole world."

Counsels on Manner of Governing. These too are highly important but also evident. The canon does not explicitly contain the profitable counsel for the superior to consult his community at times, in matters, and in a manner that are appropriate and productive. The canon, as Vatican II, states that the superior retains his authority. It is he or she who governs the institute, province and house.

Authoritarianism may have been a problem in the past but that past is now more than sufficiently remote. Since Vatican II the defects have been permissiveness and almost no government by superiors and the at least implicit exclusion of government by those supposedly under the superiors. Communities have been allowed to flow down the stream and finally to touch the bottom in secularism. John Paul II stated the evident principle that both authoritarianism and weakness are to be avoided by superiors.

623. *Interval of Final or Definitive Profession Before Becoming Superior*. The former canon law required perpetual vows and 35 years of

age for a general superior, 30 years for all other high superiors. A private reply of June 9, 1976, advised the constitutional prescription also of a number of years of final profession for the office of general superioress. No qualities were enjoined in common law for local superiors.

The present can. 623 requires that the passage of a suitable period of time in the institute after perpetual or definitive profession be determined by proper law for the election or appointment of a superior but by the constitutions for major superiors. The interval in the institute is determined by institute law; its necessity for the validity of the designation is by and from canon law.

I believe that at least 35 years is the suitable age for the general superior and at least 30 years for all other superiors, inclusive of minor local superiors. 35 is the preceding norm for the general superior, 30 for all other higher superiors, and 30 was also the very common norm for minor local superiors in constitutions approved by the Holy See. The suitable interval in the institute would be then at least 10 years for the general superior and 5 for all other superiors.

An institute must determine the desirable age for superiors and then deduce the suitable interval in the institute after perpetual or definitive profession. The phrase, "in the institute," excludes the computation of the time of perpetual or definitive profession in another institute from which a member had transferred. This has been the sense of such a requirement, e.g., in the 1917 can. 559 regarding the years of profession demanded for a master and assistant master of novices. Therefore, the omission of "in the institute" from the final text of the present can. 623 does not change its sense.

The canon distinguishes *perpetual* from *definitive* profession for institutes of only temporary vows. In these a temporary profession after a determined period of years was likened to a perpetual profession and was called a definitive profession. The period of time in the previous law was at least commonly six years (see *Sedes Sapientiae*, art. 8, § 1, 2° - 3°). Since the usual length of temporary profession may be from three to six years, I believe that a definitive profession under the new canon law should also be at least six years. The determined period is to be established in the institute law of all institutes of only temporary vows.

624, § 1. *Determined Term of Office*. All superiors are to be given a determined term of office by the proper law, for example, three or six years. This duration is to be appropriate to the nature and needs of an institute. However, a general superior or the superior of an autonomous monastery or house may be designated for an indefinite period, for example, until he is replaced by the general or monastery chapter, or for life.

I myself shudder at the thought of a local superior for life but this is not excluded by the canon. I had grown into the principle that the closer a superior is to those governed the shorter should be his term of office, which is evidently not accepted by the canon. Part of the specification of a term of office in proper law should be the limitation of reappointment and re-election, for example, not beyond an immediate second term. Religious should study carefully and conscientiously the modern practice given below. According to the present canon, they may establish any length of terms; any, indefinite or no immediate reappointment or re-election, even though the total consecutive duration to be prescribed according to § 2 is restrictive of the total time in office.

§ 2. *Excessive Consecutive Time in Office*. This paragraph extends to all superiors who have a determined term of office and also therefore to general superiors and superiors of autonomous houses who have a determined term. The canon enacts that suitable norms are to be established in proper law to prevent such superiors from remaining ''too long without interruption in offices of government.''

I believe an interval of one or two years is sufficient because the dearth of members capable of governing at least satisfactorily must also be considered. The canon extends only to excessive consecutive time in office, for example, twelve years or more as local superior in one or more houses. It should be forbidden in proper law that he or she be immediately designated local superior in any house before the expiration of the prescribed interval. The practical difficulty has been the constant and almost universal reappointment immediately of local superiors to other houses.

I do not believe the law extends to different levels of government, e.g., the local superior just described could immediately be designated as general or provincial superior with full eligibility; a provincial superior who has reached the limited number of years in one or more provinces could not be immediately designated as provincial in any other province but could be made general or local superior. Otherwise complicated cases will occur. I believe that a general superior on reaching the limit could be immediately made a provincial or local superior. General and provincial superiors on their own level can be prevented from an excessive time in office by limiting the number of their immediate re-elections or reappointments. The law has been established not only for the good of the institute but also for that of superiors. All circumstances must be considered in interpreting canon 624, § 2. A like limitation of reappointment or re-election could be established for local superiors and those of autonomous houses.

Practice of the Holy See. The practice of the Holy See in approving constitutions has been opposed to a very long duration in office for any major superiors and to the repeated and immediate re-election or reappointment of the same person, especially in institutes of women. The latest practice had been to assign the general superior a term of six years, to permit an immediate re-election for a second term of six years, but postulation was required for a third and further term. The Holy See was not favorable to postulation. A postulation of a major superior who was at the head of a monastery of nuns for a third or fourth successive three-year term was usually granted, but only with difficulty for a third successive term of six years or a second of twelve years of a general superior in pontifical centralized institutes, and most rarely and only for compelling reasons for a fourth successive term.

The principal reason for postulation is the lack of another member capable for the office. After he has been out of office for any length of time whatever, a former general superior regains full eligibility for the office, that is, he has the same eligibility as if he had never been general superior. The same principle was true of the election and appointment of any other major superior and also of minor local superiors. Such an interval is verified when another has held the office, no matter for how brief a period of time. Constitutions sometimes required a longer and determined period of time out of office, e.g., six years for the general superior, three or six years for the provincial, and one, three, or six years for a minor local superior. A founder has no right to retain the office of general superior for life contrary to constitutions defining the term of office and forbidding the immediate re-election of the same person beyond a certain limit.

In approving constitutions, the Holy See permitted provincials only two successive three-year terms, sometimes three such terms, in the same province. A few institutes had a six-year term but permitted only a second immediate term. The same two terms were the practice for the superiors of autonomous monasteries of nuns, but the duration of the term has been three years. The same norm of only two immediate terms was the practice for presidents of federations and confederations of such autonomous houses. The duration of the term was six years.

By reason of can. 505, a minor local superior as such could not be given a term of office beyond three years, but a second immediate term in the same house was permitted. Whatever the length of the term, the same local superior was not permitted to govern the same house for more than six successive years. An apparent exception to this norm was permitted when the first term was partial, e.g., two years. A second three-year term was evidently permissible and also a third because the superior did not have two complete previous terms. The canon did not forbid the immediate reappointment as superior of another house after the completion of the permissible time in one house.

Miscellanea on Superiors. Some institutes demand a two-thirds vote for the first or subsequent elections of major superiors; a few forbid any postulation. The new can. 181, § 1 requires at least a two-thirds majority for any postulation. Religious are now familiar with the distinction between a superior and a member put over only the work of a house, such as the president of a college, administrator of a hospital, the principal of a school, and so forth. They also realize that a canon such as can. 624, § 2 applies only to religious superiors as such. The duration of a term, unless law established otherwise, is computed according to can. 203, § 2, i.e., a three-year term begun on January 10, 1980 expires at midnight of January 10-11, 1983.

The constitutions, customs, usage or practice usually specify that the term of an appointive office begins and that of the predecessor ends on the day the appointed member assumes office. Only a small number of institutes establish that the term begins to run from the date of the letter of appointment. A few constitutions enact that a superior's term expiring within the school year is automatically prolonged until the end of the school year. Some institutes automatically prolong the term of local and provincial superiors, expiring after the convocation of the general chapter, until the close of this, or for the local superiors, of the provincial chapter.

Likewise, according to the constitutions, customs, practice or usage, a superior on the expiration of his term continues to govern until his own repeated designation or that of his successor is effective. Otherwise, even if this power is not explicitly granted in the proper law, the competent higher superior may extend the term for a proportionate reason and a brief period until the designation of the successor is effective. In all these cases the former superior governs under the title of vicar. If neither of these methods of prolongation is verified, the government passes to the assistant. However, it is a tenable opinion that the superior always continues to govern in such a case. This opinion is in conformity with the practice of the Holy See in approving constitutions.

Term of Office of Those in Charge of Filial Houses. It appertains to the constitutions to enact whether such a member is appointed for a determined term, for no determined term, and to what extent he may be immediately appointed or for how long he may continuously govern the same filial house. Several authors follow Vermeersch (*Periodica*, 17 [1928], 90*) in stating it to be the mind of the Holy See that the same member should not have this office in the same filial house for more than three successive three-year terms or more than nine successive years. This is a solid practical norm but it has not been included in all constitutions approved by the Holy See that mention filial houses.

Transfer, Removal and Resignation. It is a principle of law (see can. 190, § 2; 193, § 2) that a superior or official who has been appointed for a determined period of time may not be removed or transferred, except the transferee consents, before the expiration of that period unless for a just and serious reason. Such reasons are the need of the member in another important post, his serious incompetency, bad example, and excessive severity or weakness. From the law of the constitutions, custom, or usage, the more common practice in religious institutes has been that an appointed superior or official, e.g., a provincial or local superior, may not resign his office but has only the right of representation, i.e., of proposing reasons to be relieved of his office. Some constitutions expressly grant provincial and local superiors the right of resigning. If resignation is neither granted nor excluded in the law or usage of an institute, a superior has the right of resigning (can. 187). It is forbidden to make or accept a resignation without a just and proportionate reason (can. 187; 189, § 2).

The authority competent for the transfer, removal or acceptance of the resignation of a provincial or local superior is ordinarily the general superior with the consent of his council, after a request for a local superior by the provincial superior with the same vote of his council. Some constitutions give this right to the latter, but the act must be confirmed by the general superior with the consent of his council. The sufficient reasons for removal and transfer should be established in proper law. (can. 624, § 3).

625, §§ 1-2. *Election of the General Superior.* The canon states as a fact that the general superior of a pontifical or diocesan institute is to be designated by an election according to the norms of canon law and the constitutions. An election in these cases, as also of the superior of an autonomous house or of a federation or confederation of autonomous houses, is practically necessary from the nature of these offices. Otherwise an appointment would have to be made by the Holy See. Canon law does not give the diocesan bishop the power of appointing superiors in diocesan institutes. In the new canons the diocesan bishop of the principal house presides, without the right of confirmation, only at the election of the general superior of a diocesan institute of men and women and of the superior of an autonomous monastery of nuns described in can. 615, whose president is evidently its own diocesan bishop.

In the present practice, the religious assistant presides at the election of the president of a federation or confederation of nuns. Priests are not the tellers at the election of the superior in a monastery of nuns. It has been the constant understanding of the law and insistence of the SCRSI that such elections must be in chapter and demand a system of delegates in centralized institutes and in federations and confederations.

§ 3. *Other Major Superiors.* These are in fact provincial superiors. The other possible major superiors must be elected, as explained in the preceding paragraph. Provincials are to be appointed by the general superior, with the consent of his council, after ample and appropriate consultation. This should also be the norm for regional superiors. Provincials may be elected in a provincial chapter, without direct vote and with a system of delegates. The election in a provincial chapter had been the practice of relatively few institutes, but the number grew during the experimental period following Vatican II. If election is the manner of designation by proper law, the election must be confirmed by the general superior. The constitutions should require the consent of the general council for this confirmation, as is again obvious from the importance of the act. Confirmation is demanded for the validity of an election (can. 179, § 4). The practice of the Holy See required in the constitutions the same confirmation for the election of the provincial councilors, secretary and treasurer and for the provincial enactments of the provincial chapter when it possessed this power.

Designation of Minor Local Superiors. These have ordinarily been appointed by the general superior with the consent of his council, even in institutes divided into provinces. In a small number of institutes, they were appointed by the provincial with the consent of his council, but the appointment had to be confirmed by the general superior with the consent of his council. The appointment of those at the head of filial houses may be regulated by the same norms or left to the provincial with the consent of his council. Can. 625, § 3 commands an apt consultation, of at least some outside the council, before the appointment of provincials or minor local superiors. If elected, minor local superiors must also be confirmed by the competent higher superior, who will be the general or provincial superior with the consent of his council.

Qualities Requisite in Superiors. It is evident that a proposed superior should possess the qualities demanded by the nature of the office and the circumstances of the particular superiorship. The practice of the SCRSI forbids a general or provincial superior to be also local superior except in a house destined solely for general or provincial officials. The constitutions may prescribe qualities for the valid or licit appointment or election of superiors but in fact they should be only for liceity. Invalidating laws are not necessary under this heading, and such laws should not be multiplied without necessity.

626. *Proper Motivation in Appointments and Elections. Exact Observance of Laws on Election. Election of the Truly Worthy and Better Qualified, and Abstention From All Abuses and Especially From the Procuring of Votes.* The order of motives in an appointment or election should be God, the Church, the greater good of the whole institute, and of the particular province or house in a provincial or house designation. The observance of universal and proper law is evidently incumbent on all; laws impose an obligation. However, there is frequently a strong temptation to violate laws on election, especially in the matter of procuring votes. The natural law itself, because of the harm that can befall the institute, imposes an obligation in conscience of designating a worthy or capable person.

The obligation of the canon is to take the means to designate the truly worthy and capable. The norm in act, particularly for a religious, should be to designate one who is, all things properly considered, the most capable for the office at the particular time. This demands constant and sincere prayer, pure motives, prudent study and reflection, investigation, and the repelling of very quick attractions and repulsions—which is one sufficiently solid reason, among many, of not holding important elections at the very beginning of a chapter. If the previous voting proves to an elector that the one he judges most qualified has no chance of being elected, it is better for him to shift his vote. It is rarely reasonable to continue to vote for an evidently hopeless candidate. It is never permitted to vote for an unworthy candidate, but it is obligatory to vote for a less worthy candidate to prevent the election of one who is unworthy.

Electioneering (Procuring of Votes). All members of an institute, whether electors or not, are forbidden to seek votes to elect a particular person, or one rather than another, or to exclude anyone from being elected by the chapter. It is forbidden to do this directly, i.e., to seek the votes openly and clearly, or indirectly, i.e., to seek votes in a secret, disguised or mediate fashion, e.g., by artifices, insinuations, favors, services, or promises. It is certainly forbidden to procure votes for an evil end, e.g., to elect an unworthy person, by evil means such as fraud, lies, threats, violence, insistent pleadings, pacts, agreements, commands of superiors, or any means that restricts the liberty of the electors. Merely to counsel another to vote or not to vote for someone presupposes accurate knowledge of the facts, an uprightness of purpose and a prudent consideration of all the circumstances.

Some authors hold with probability that the canon does not forbid procuring votes provided the end and the means are licit in themselves, e.g., to induce another by sound reasons and from honest motives to vote for the best qualified, for a better rather than a less qualified person, or for a qualified rather than an unqualified person. The more common opinion is that this procuring also is forbidden because the wording of the canon is absolute, as in the past. The latter opinion should be followed in practice since any procuring of votes is apt to cause factions, create parties determined on their candidate, produce bad feelings, and disturb the peace and sanctity of the religious life. The procuring of votes does not invalidate a vote or an election bcause the canon does not contain an invalidating clause.

Preliminary Discussions. A private or public discussion among the capitulars on the merits and demerits of particular persons for the offices to which the elections are to be made is not mentioned in canon law and consequently is neither commanded nor forbidden by the canons. The constitutions often contain a statement that prudent consultation regarding the qualifications of those eligible is permitted within the bounds of justice and charity (see RfR, 23 [1964], 226-29).

Such consultations are at least very frequently necessary. The capitulars of the United States, for example, will rarely know the members of England, France or Germany who have the qualifications necessary for a general superior. This is almost equally true of any large institute or province. In a house or a small institute or province, such consultations will not be generally necessary, but even in these, some individual electors will find it necessary to consult and seek information on those qualified. It is also true even in smaller institutes that those of one age level, locality or field of work are often ignorant of the abilities and accomplishments of those of other levels, localities and fields of labor.

It is rarely expedient and profitable to hold such discussions publicly in an assembly of the capitulars. They should consist of private discussions among a few or of individual consultations. These consultations are to be limited to a sincere seeking and giving of information on the abilities and deficiencies of particular persons insofar as this is necessary or useful for judging whether the person is suitable for the office in question. The common and greater good of the institute, province or house should be the motive. All motives of mere personal friendship or aversion, of pushing a member because he is from one's own province or country, as also and especially of forming blocs or parties, are clearly out of place.

Nominating Ballot. A nominating ballot, especially one made by the whole institute or province, can be of some help, but it should not be taken as an infallible or obligatory norm. It is always understood that the chapter members may vote for religious who were not nominated. The capitulars are the electors, not those who are not members of the chapter.

627. *Necessity and Purpose of a Council.* The canon obliges all general, provincial and local superiors of canonically erected houses to have their own council. From the enactments of particular constitutions or statutes, the president of federations and confederations, of vice-provinces, quasi-provinces, regions, vicariates, missions and districts frequently

also has councilors. The canon leaves to the constitutions the specification of the smaller houses that do not require a council or whose council will consist of a smaller number. In the 1917 code, a council was required "at least in formal houses," which consisted of at least six professed religious. Nor does the following provision of the letter of the secretary of the SCRSI, July 10, 1972, appear incompatible with the canon:"There is nothing to prevent the entire community from being members of the local council, especially in small houses. But in larger communities, the usual type of council would be necessary, particularly when rather delicate matters must be discussed; however in other items of general interest the consultation of the entire local community is to be favored."

Number of Councilors. Can. 627 does not specify the number of councilors. In the practice of the Holy See in approving constitutions, there were four general councilors, although some institutes had a greater number; four or two provincial councilors; two councilors in a formal house, but some institutes had a larger number, and more frequently one councilor in a small house. Autonomous houses ordinarily had four councilors, which was also the ordinary norm of federations and confederations.

Manner of Designation and Requisite Qualities of Councilors. The general councilors and those of a federation, confederation or autonomous house are elected in the respective chapters. The provincial councilors are appointed by the general superior with the consent of his council but in some institutes they are elected in the provincial chapter. Local councilors are appointed by the general superior or by the provincial with the consent of the respective council. The constitutions sometimes enact that the latter appointment is to be confirmed by the general superior with the deliberative vote of his council. Local councilors may also be elected or nominated by the local community.

The quality universally demanded by constitutions in the past for all except local councilors was that they were to be professed of perpetual vows. The age usually required for general councilors was thirty-five, thirty for the councilors of a federation, confederation and autonomous houses; thirty or thirty-five years were often prescribed for provincial councilors. The constitutions rarely enacted a determined age for local councilors, and very many did not affirm that perpetual vows were necessary. A few made it clear that perpetual profession was not an absolute requisite by stating that local councilors were, "if possible," to be of perpetual vows or that such vows were required at least for the first councilor.

Residence. According to the past practice of the Holy See in approving constitutions, all the general councilors had to reside with the general superior; but two of them, with the exception of the assistant general, could live elsewhere for a just reason, e.g., because of their other work. These had to be stationed in houses from which they could be readily summoned and could attend council meetings. The evident purpose of the practice was that the general superior would have no difficulty in consulting his councilors. The greater facility of travel renders such a law unnecessary in very many institutes.

Many constitutions contained no enactment on the residence of the provincial councilors. Some constitutions had the same practice for a provincial council of four members as that described above for the general council. If there were only two provincial councilors, the constitutions frequently stated that both or at least one of the councilors must reside with the provincial. The councilors of a federation or confederation reside in their respective monasteries. It seems to be a more practical norm for many institutes that only one councilor, usually the assistant, should be obliged to reside with the general and provincial superiors. The councilors can then be assigned to other general, provincial or local duties according to their abilities and the need of the institute or province. This will often be a means of properly employing the councilors and of giving them a work-life in which they can have satisfaction.

Incompatible Duties. The general principle of the practice of the Holy See forbade a general councilor to be assigned any employment that would prevent the proper fulfillment of the duties of a councilor. The more recent practice forbade in particular merely that the first councilor be general treasurer or secretary. The judgment on incompatibility is to be made on facts, i.e., the amount of work in each of the offices and the ease or difficulty with which the other office would permit the member to be summoned and to attend the ordinary and extraordinary sessions of the general council.

Nature of a Council. In the constitutions the general council is frequently stated to consist of the general superior and the four general councilors. All such expressions are ambiguous. The superior alone governs the institute, province or house; the councilors as such have no authority. Canon law, which attributes authority only to superiors and chapters, makes it clear that a councilor is only an advisor of a superior, not an associate in authority. The superior votes in a council but is not a member of a council; he is the superior, or sole possessor of authority, who has councilors or advisors.

In a general chapter the authority is that of the collective body: the chapter itself and as such possesses the authority. All the members of the chapter are on the same level; all are co-possessors of the same authority and co-authors of the enactments of the chapter. Not the presiding general superior, but the general chapter places an act. A council is not a governing body; it of itself possesses no collective authority. The councilors are not co-authors of an act. It is not the council but the superior who places an act with the consent or advice of his council. On the fact that the superior also votes in a council, see Tabera-Antonana-Escudero, *Il diritto dei religiosi*, no. 118, 3; Bastien, *Directoire-Canonique*, no. 326; Escudero, *Il nuovo diritto dei religiosi*, p. 82, note 82, and others. Gutierrez, CpR, 54 (1973), 129-33 holds the contrary opinion.

It is possible for a canon or a norm of the constitutions to prescribe that, in a particular matter, the council is to act in the same way as the general chapter, i.e., in a completely collegial manner. This must be proved certainly, since the contrary is the general principle of canon law. It should be done only in a few cases in which the general council substitutes for the general chapter, or in matters that are highly important and distinctive e.g., in the appointment of a general councilor in the vacancy of this office. Otherwise, the council would lose its nature of being an advisory, not a governing, body. These same principles apply not only to the councils but also to the chapters in autonomous houses in the cases for which law demands that the superior secure the consent or advice of the chapter. In deciding affairs, such a chapter is on the same level as a council. Whether the matter is of canon or proper law, acting as a council is the ordinary manner, acting in a purely collegial way is the exceptional (see RfR, 36 [1977], 480).

Duties of Councilors. The primary duty of the councilors is to give a deliberative or consultative vote when either is demanded by canon law, the constitutions or the directory. When asked to do so by the superior, they are to express their opinion with all sincerity. They are likewise to bring to the attention of the superior whatever they sincerely consider to be to the good or detriment of the institute, province or house. However, the superior, not the councilors, decides the matters that are to be treated in the council, since he is the one possessing authority. Councils were introduced to prevent what could degenerate into arbitrary government by the superior. An equally evident purpose was to satisfy the need that all, and perhaps especially those in authority, have of securing advice and of learning the facts necessary for a prudent judgment and decision. The councilors should also be a rich source of truly progressive ideas to the superior.

Obligation of Secrecy. According to the past practice of the Holy See, an article of the constitutions stated that the general councilors must observe secrecy concerning all matters confided to them as councilors in or outside of the sessions. Another article usually included in constitutions extended the same obligation to all others who attended any session of the general council. The new can. 127, § 3 states, "and if the importance of affairs demands it, [they have the obligation] of faithfully observing secrecy, and this obligation may be urged by the superior."

A *secret* is the knowledge of something that at least ordinarily should not be revealed. A *natural secret* arises from the matter itself of such knowledge, since its revelation would cause injury or at least sorrow and displeasure to another. A *promised secret* has its source in a promise, made after the matter was known, not to reveal this matter, whether or not the matter of itself demands secrecy. The *confided or entrusted secret* arises from an agreement, given and accepted before any disclosure, that the matter will not be revealed. The agreement may be either explicit or implicit. The latter is true of all who hold a confidential office, e.g., doctors, lawyers, priests consulted outside of confession on things appertaining to their ministry, superiors in institutes of consecrated life, novice directors, councilors, and so forth.

There are degrees in the confided secret. The lowest is the revelation made to a private individual from mere friendship. The next is the revelation to a private individual to secure counsel. The third and highest is the official secret, i.e., a revelation made to a person possessing a confidential office, such as those listed above, and made because of or learned in the performance of the office. Important matters in the judgment of the superior and confided to one or all councilors thus constitute official secrets and are often also natural secrets. Evidently unimportant matters can still be secret matter, especially as a natural or confided secret.

Even the official secret may be revealed to prevent serious harm to the institute, a province or house, or to any individual. The councilors may also reveal such matters to a prudent and learned or experienced person for the purpose of consultation, e.g., a confessor, a priest learned or skilled in a subject such as canon law or moral theology, or to another prudent and experienced person. The identity of the person concerned is to be concealed as far as possible. If a matter becomes public, the councilors may not reveal what occurred in the council concerning it, e.g., the opinions or votes given by individual councilors.

Frequency of Sessions. The almost universal practice of the SCRSI in approving constitutions has been that an ordinary session of the general council is to be held every month. More frequent sessions are to be convoked when necessary. A very small number of institutes prescribed less frequent meetings, e.g., every two or three months. It is very difficult to reconcile such infrequent sessions with the obligation of having all the councilors reside in the motherhouse and with the insistence that they be free of all duties incompatible with the office of general councilor. An ordinary session every month is the preferable norm. An extraordinary session should be convoked by the general superior for any matter of greater moment. He should consult his council frequently, since the practice of the SCRSI places marked emphasis on the office of councilor.

These principles are true of all other councils. A monthly ordinary session is also the usual norm of provinces and houses. The frequency of the meetings of the chapter and council in autonomous houses is likely to manifest a greater variety. Local community meetings and provincial assemblies are recent innovations on the counseling level. The same is true of enlarged general councils composed of the general superior, general council, general treasurer and secretary, provincials, vice-provincials, as well as other individuals as observers or experts and selected according to determined criteria. Some of these meet annually or every two years. There can be similar bodies varying with the institute.

Convocation of a Council. When either the deliberative or consultative vote is required by canon law, the constitutions or directory, can. 127, § 1 commands the superior to convoke all the councilors (see can. 166, § 1), unless proper law establishes otherwise regarding counsel only. The superior, sufficiently ahead of time, must inform all the councilors of the place, day and hour of the session. Such a convocation is not necessary when the proper law or customs determine the place, day and hour of the meetings. If more than a third were not convoked the act of the superior is invalid, unless all who were overlooked were actually present (can. 166, § 3). The secretary may and often in fact does convoke the council at the order of the superior. The councilors should at the same time be given a list of the important matters to be discussed, so that they may properly prepare for the session. Unprepared sessions are usually unsatisfactory and unduly prolonged.

Number of Councilors Required. The canon directly on a council, 127, does not require a determined number of councilors to be present, which however may be enacted by proper law. Most constitutions, following the *Normae* of 1901, no. 273, required a full general council for appointments to office. A small number extended this to other matters, e.g., admission to the first and final professions, dismissal of professed members, matters that demanded recourse to the Holy See or the local ordinary, and even for all matters that required a deliberative vote. Full membership was required in such constitutions for the liceity, not the validity, of the act of the superior.

Constitutions approved by the Holy See usually contained a norm of substitution for an absent general councilor, e.g., that the substitute should be the general treasurer or secretary, or that the general superior should choose a member of definitive or perpetual vows as substitute. Such norms may also be followed by other institutes that lack a norm of substitution (can. 19). Constitutions rarely mentioned the necessity of a full provincial council for determined matters or gave norms of substitution for this council. Such provisions, when found, followed those described above for the general council.

Non-councilors Attending Sessions. The constitutions usually stated, at least of the general superior, that he might summon members who are not councilors to sessions of the council to give information and advice but that he is forbidden to grant a vote to anyone who is not a councilor. Any superior has this same right, also with regard to externs.

Procedure. The councilors should have been previously informed of the matters to be discussed so that these could be properly studied. They should have been given a similar opportunity of submitting their own proposals for discussion. The superior proposes the matters for discussion. He should give an objective description of each case when necessary, without revealing his own opinion. He then asks the opinion of each of the councilors. The superior is to strive to secure a sincere and complete expression of opinion from all the councilors. Can. 127, § 3 obliges the councilors to express their opinions sincerely.

The superior should take care lest any more aggressive and vocal members dominate the council. These are not necessarily the most able or prudent. The councilors are to consider all matters objectively; they are not to be motivated by partisanship, factionalism, anger, pride, stubbornness, or blind adherence to their own opinions. The councilors have full liberty to express their opinions. Their norm is the objective merits or demerits of the matter, not merely what the superior wants. To assure this liberty, it is better that the superior give his opinion last. The superior must be careful lest his attitude intimidate or discourage the councilors from a sincere expression of opinion. He obviously may never in fact consider the council as a mere "rubber stamp" for his own ideas.

The amount of time given to each matter will evidently vary with its importance and the ease or difficulty in reaching a decision. The superior determines the duration and the number of times each councilor is to speak. Some constitutions state that an interval is to be allowed, at least on the petition of the majority of the council, between the session in which a matter is proposed and that in which it is to be decided, unless the matter is urgent. This will ordinarily occur only in important matters, but it is a norm that prudence itself will frequently demand or counsel. Some constitutions specify the interval as of one day or more, three or more, and three or eight days.

Manner of Voting. Can. 127 does not impose any determined manner of voting, i.e., orally, in writing, publicly or secretly. Very few constitutions contain any provision on the manner of voting, even though the *Normae* of 1901 stated that the deliberative vote was to be secret (no. 273). The varying provisions on the necessity of a secret vote in constitutions were: for all matters; whenever the deliberative vote is required; only for appointments; councilors may request it for an important matter, and when demanded by canon law, by the constitutions, or when requested by two councilors. The preferable norm is a secret vote whenever the deliberative vote is required.

Necessity of Voting. Whenever the deliberative vote is required, the councilors are actually to vote, and the result of the voting is to be announced to the council. Otherwise the superior could not be certain that he had the consent of the council. The superior also votes. Actual voting may be done but is not necessary when only the advice or consultative vote is demanded. The superior is not obliged to follow even a unanimous consultative vote, and he can reach his decision merely from the opinions proposed by the councilors.

Number of Votes Required (can. 127, § 1). Affairs and appointments are decided by can. 127, § 1. For the validity of the consent of a council, this canon demands that the matter receive the approval of the absolute majority of the members present. Only one ballot is required by can. 127, § 1. Nothing is said in the canon on the norm of breaking a tie. This norm (see can. 19) is the same as that for collegial acts in can. 119, 2°, i.e., the superior may break the tie by his vote. For the validity of a required advice or consultative vote, it is sufficient that the superior have sought the advice of *all* his councilors either in or outside of a common deliberation, e.g., by individual approach or letter.

Deliberative and Consultative Vote. Deliberative Vote. There is no ambiguity in the expression of the deliberative vote. It is required whenever common law or the constitutions demand the consent or deliberative or decisive vote of a council or chapter. The necessity of this vote is also perfectly clear from can. 127, § 1, i.e., a superior acts invalidly when he acts without or contrary to the majority vote in any matter for which the deliberative vote is required.

An important distinction is to be kept in mind. Let us take as an example the canonical erection of a house for which the constitutions require the deliberative vote of the general council. The general superior is not obliged to propose or to admit the proposal of this matter, since it appertains to the superior to determine whether a particular matter is to be submitted to the council. If he does propose it, the general superior must have the consent of his council to erect the house validly. If he secures this consent, he may erect the house but he is not obliged to do so. He may abstain from such an action. The law commands him to *have* the consent of his council to erect the house; it does not oblige him to act *according to the consent* of his council, as would be the case in a completely collegial act, e.g., an enactment of the general chapter.

Consultative Vote. This means that a superior is to listen to the opinions of his council. It is clearly stated in the following expressions: "with the consultative vote," "with the advice of the council," "having consulted" or "heard" the council, and "according to the counsel" or "advice" of the council. The expression "with the vote of the council" or "with the council" is thought by some to be ambiguous but is to be interpreted in itself as demanding only a consultative vote. Since the necessity of a vote is restrictive of the right of a superior, the requirement is to be interpreted strictly. Therefore, if it is doubtful whether the vote imposed is deliberative or consultative, it is only consultative; and if it is doubtful whether any vote is necessary, no vote is necessary (can. 18). Ambiguous expressions should be avoided in constitutions.

No Obligation to Follow the Consultative Vote. The code does not oblige a superior to follow even the unanimous consultative vote of his council but he is advised ordinarily to do so, i.e., he should not depart from their vote unless he has a reason that prevails over the vote (see can. 127, § 2, 2°). It is evident that a superior is always to give due consideration to the advice of his council especially, but not only, when it is unanimous; otherwise the office of a councilor and the obligation of seeking advice in such matters would be mere formalities.

Matters That Require a Deliberative or Consultative Vote. The source of such a requisite is common law or the proper law of an institute. This necessity or recommendation is indicated here in the treatment of each matter.

Minutes. There should be a council book, in which the minutes of each session are recorded by the secretary. These are to contain the date, names of the absentees and of any substitutes, all affairs that were discussed, the decisions reached, and the number of votes for and against each decision. The minutes are approved by the council at the beginning of the following session, with a notation of the numbers of the votes of this approval. The minutes are then signed by the superior and the secretary or, according to some constitutions, by all the councilors. In many institutes the minutes are signed before the approval of the council. There are also institutes in which this approval is not prescribed. The reading and approval of the minutes are an ordinary practice in both secular and religious bodies of this nature.

127, § 2. *Case Not Included in the 1917 Code.* This occurs when a superior is obliged by law to secure the consent or advice of *some persons as individuals*, not of a college or group as in the case of a council. These persons may be one or several, equals, inferiors, or superiors in authority. The act of the superior is invalid if he did not seek the prescribed consent or advice of the designated persons. The action of the superior requiring consent is invalid, secondly, if it was contrary to the vote of all or any one of such persons.

All such designated persons have the same obligations of giving their opinion sincerely and of secrecy as explained above for a college or group (can. 127, § 3). Although only ''some persons'' are explicitly mentioned in can. 127, § 2, it seems to me that the canon applies fully when there is only one designated person whose consent or advice is to be secured, e.g., when the law commands that the consent of the diocesan bishop be secured. This is also the usual type of case that occurs in fact.

628, § 1. *Obligation of Making Visitations.* Visitations are made by major superiors, particularly by general and provincial superiors of centralized institutes, as also by presidents of federations and confederations. This canon obliges those designated in the constitutions for visitations to perform this duty with regard to houses and members and to observe the other norms of the constitutions on visitations. The frequency of visitations of the general superior, personally or by delegate, in institutes approved by the Holy See, has been more commonly every three years, or at least once in a six-year term. Many institutes not divided into provinces had a greater frequency of every second year, at least every second year, or annually. By far the greater number of institutes imposed an annual visitation by the provincial; a small number limited this obligation to one visitation in three years or two in three years.

The annual visitation is the much more preferable norm, and it may always be made, even when not commanded by the constitutions. The general superior may also make more frequent visitations than those commanded by the constitutions. It is the common interpretation and is sometimes stated in the constitutions that the provincial superior is not obliged or should not visit a house during a year in which it has been or is to be visited by the general superior or his delegate. The provincial visitation could impede the effectiveness of that of the general superior. Furthermore, it is not prudent to burden a community with too many visitations. If the particular constitutions do not impose a visitation, the higher superior has no obligation but always has the right of making a visitation. Some constitutions do not oblige the general superior to make visitations but this would be unthinkable for a provincial and also for a general superior of an institute not divided into provinces.

Centralized institutes can also have vice-provinces, quasi-provinces, regions, missions, districts and vicariates, which should as a general principle follow the same norms and frequency as those of provinces. The latest norm of the Holy See is that presidents of federations and confederations may make a "friendly" visitation of autonomous houses once during a six-year term. The usual norm of constitutions permits a general superior to designate a visitor for a particular matter or an individual house but demands the consent of the general council for the delegation of a visitor for the entire institute if this visitor is not a member of the general council. Some constitutions extended the necessity of this consent to any delegated visitor for the institute and to a visitor delegated by the general superior for an entire province. The same norm ordinarily regulated the necessity of the consent of his council in the delegation of a visitor by the provincial superior.

Purpose of Visitation. The primary purpose is to investigate and promote proper religious living and to correct deficiencies. This purpose implies the encouragement of the fervent, the prudent correction of delinquents, and the prescribing of means apt to restore, preserve and increase the proper religious life. Prudent government does not exclude decisive action when this is demanded by the circumstances. The major superior is also to learn the spiritual and temporal needs and desires of members and to grant these according to the sound principles of the religious life, the common good, and that of the individual. The purpose of the visitation is also to investigate the government of provincial and local superiors and the administration of the temporal property of the house and province.

Defects of government and administration are to be prudently corrected, but the members should not think that the one purpose of a visitation interview is to give a criticism of the government. An important purpose of a visitation is that the higher superior acquires a deeper knowledge of the current capabilities and deficiencies of the members. This should be of notable assistance in making the appointments for both the common and individual good. The visitation extends to all things, e.g., the furnishing of the house, the chapel, sacristy, the proper care of the sick, the clothing, heating, light, food, the book of minutes of the council, and, not the least, to the library, which is often an accurate measure of the intellectual life of the community. The success of the work of the community and of its relation to those outside the community is obviously an important aspect of the visitation.

The Field of a Visitation. This is the field of religious government as opposed to that of conscience. The former consists of all conduct of a religious that is external and knowable to others. A manifestation of conscience in the strict and proper sense is the revelation by a member to a superior of his own actions that are completely interior or external but not knowable to others, provided either is the type of action that one would not care to reveal to another except under a pledge of secrecy.

Superiors may legitimately question a subject about matters appertaining to personal conduct under the field of religious government, and the subject is obliged to answer truthfully, provided the superior is interrogating the subject in the manner that is called paternal, not as the head of the community. If he interrogates under the latter formality, the obligation of replying truthfully is restricted to the case in which the offense is proved and such proof has been demonstrated to the subject. The superior interrogates in a paternal manner when he intends the spiritual good, the paternal correction of a member, e.g., to admonish, reprehend, or to impose a penance that is not defamatory. He inquires as the head of the community when he intends the punishment of the member or the common good, e.g., by the dismissal of the member.

Investigation of religious discipline by superiors is of two types, general and special. A general investigation is an inquiry into the common observance of the norms of the religious life and into the commission of faults that harm the community or the spiritual progress of individuals. This may always be made by superiors, since it is part of their duty of promoting the good of the community and of individuals. A special investigation is one made about a determined individual. This should not be done unless it rests on a founded rumor or suspicion of the misconduct of the individual. Justice and charity require that a suspicion should not be admitted unless it rests on a probable foundation and that the reputation of an individual should not be imprudently damaged.

Denunciation. Denunciation is the technical term that signifies the revealing of the conduct of a companion to a superior. Members do not and should not reveal the petty and purely personal defects of companions. This is to be classified as talebearing. Members may certainly reveal to a superior the faults and defects of companions that are of no great malice but are distracting, annoying, disturbing, interfere with one's own work, rest, peace or happiness, with that of others, or of the entire community, e.g., the making of noise that disturbs the sleep of others. A superior may inquire, and members are obliged to answer truthfully, about an offense of a companion if there exists a founded suspicion of the commission of the offense by the particular member, or if a truthful answer is necessary to avoid the danger of serious harm to the institute, province, the house, an innocent third party, or the delinquent himself. Ordinarily at least, members should be advised to reveal the latter type of matter spontaneously.

Use of Knowledge Acquired in a Visitation. The purpose of the visitation is not mere spiritual direction but government, and evidently gives the visitor the right of using what he has learned in the visitation. The visitor may therefore do such things as instruct, reprehend, correct, change the employment, office, or house of a member because of what he has learned in a visitation. In the use of information that is not commonly known in the community, the visitor is to be careful to protect the reputation of the member. He is forbidden to use, outside of the interview itself, anything learned in a voluntary manifestation of conscience without the express consent of the one who made the manifestation.

Revelation of Things Learned in a Visitation. To reveal is to tell others. In general the visitor is forbidden to reveal secret matters learned in a visitation. This obligation of secrecy clearly does not extend to matters that are commonly known in the community, but a prudent superior avoids indiscriminate conversation on personal matters that even *appear* to have been learned in virtue of his office. He is to conceal the identity of the one who gave the information. The visitor may reveal secret matters learned in a visitation to a higher superior or to his councilors if this is judged necessary for a more permanent and effective correction. It is always forbidden to reveal anything learned in a manifestation of conscience without the express consent of the subject.

Instructions and Regulations. The visitation will be partially ineffective unless means are taken to further the good that the community is doing, to bring it to effect the good that is being left undone, and to correct abuses. The visitor should write out instructions on these points. It will usually be sufficient to reaffirm existing obligations without enacting new regulations for the community. According to the practice of the institute, these instructions may be the topic of the closing talk of the visitor, may be given only to the superior, who is always charged with their enforcement; or copies may be distributed to the members of the community. Defects treated in this manner should be frequent and quite common violations of the norms and principles of the religious life. Other defects are to be taken care of by individual correction. The visitor is also to strive in the instructions to further positively the spiritual life and work of the community or province and to avoid concentration on the negative aspect of the correction of defects.

§ 3. *Obligation to Respond Truthfully to a Visitor.* This obligation has been explained above. The canon also inculcates a trusting attitude towards a visitor. Evidently this trust implies that the superiors in general are faithful members of the religious life, sufficiently competent, truthful, sincere, free of factionalism and are an effective and mature aid to the individual members and to the community in general. The interference with legitimate interrogation that is prohibited to all includes what is done personally or through anyone else, whether directly, by inducing or commanding others expressly to conceal the truth, or indirectly by praise, promises, or special attention intended for the same purpose but without expressly mentioning this purpose. All are finally forbidden by the canon to hinder the purpose of the visitation in any other way.

§ 2. *Visitation by Diocesan Bishop.* It is the right and duty of the diocesan bishop to visit, also regarding religious discipline, the autonomous monasteries of nuns designated in can. 615 and all houses of a diocesan institute of men or women, also regarding religious discipline, that are located in his territory. No specific frequency of visitation is here established, but the general norm of an episcopal visitation is every five years, according to can. 396, § 1.

629. *Residence.* All superiors, general, intermediate and especially local, are obliged to reside in their own houses and not to absent themselves from these except in accord with the manner, reasons, and the time determined in proper law. This matter may also be regulated by custom, legitimate usage, or regulations of the general chapter or higher superiors.

630, § 1. *Freedom Regarding Penance and Direction of Conscience.* The canon inculcates the principle that superiors are to leave due freedom to all members in their use of the sacrament of penance and of direction of conscience, but adds that the discipline of the institute is to be observed.

§ 2. *Habitually Accessible Confessors.* Frequent confession is something that appertains as a counsel almost to the nature of the religious life. The very common definition of frequent confession has been that made at least every two weeks. The responsibility for sufficient provision of confessors is incumbent on superiors, practically therefore on the local superiors. The practicality of the priest who says the daily Mass in lay communities having the custom of hearing confessions beforehand retains all its validity in this new legislation and day. No member is to be obliged against his will to confess to a specific priest.

Paul VI recalled the attention of all, priests, religious and the faithful, to the practice of frequent confession. He also stated that a low esteem of this frequency was not the thought of the Church (*Notitiae*, 11 [1975], 222). He likewise affirmed: "moreover, with regard to the practice of frequent confession, we ask you to recall to your priests and religious and laity—to all the faithful in search of holiness—the words of our predecessor Pius XII: 'Not without the inspiration of the Holy Spirit was this practice introduced into the Church' " (AAS, 70 [1978], 331-2). John Paul II has been equally frequent and firm in his urging of frequent confession for all.

Religious can be equally unmindful of the doctrine of the Council of Trent (Denzinger, no. 899) that venial sins could be remitted in many other ways than by confession, a doctrine that can be summed up practically as follows: "For the remission of their venial sins, particularly as manifested in tolerated habits of such fully deliberate sins, they shall be attentive to sincere sorrow especially through the grace of repentance of mass, through acts of perfect love at and by the effect of Holy Communion itself, as also at the penitential rite of Mass and in their daily examination of conscience" (RfR, 37 [1978], 299).

§ 3. *Ordinary Confessors.* In monasteries of nuns, houses of formation such as novitiates and houses of study, and more numerous lay communities, ordinary confessors are to be approved by the local ordinary, after consultation with the local community, and given the faculty to hear confessions whenever this is necessary. No obligation of approaching these confessors may be imposed. The obligation of appointing extraordinary confessors no longer exists. The last class extends also to more numerous and entirely lay communities in a clerical institute. The second class of houses of formation literally may be applied also to clerical institutes. In all types of clerical institutes, confessors are designated by the religious superiors competent according to the constitutions.

§ 4. *Superiors as Confessors*. In a pontifical clerical institute of religious life, the superiors who, in accordance with their constitutions, have executive power of governing also have the faculty of hearing the confessions of their subjects and of those living day and night in the house of consecrated life. Other priest superiors can have this faculty from a higher superior or a local ordinary. Priest superiors possessing this faculty always validly hear the confessions of those named above. They are, however, forbidden by the present canon to hear the confessions of these same penitents unless the latter voluntarily request it. Having such a request, a priest superior may hear such penitents also habitually and no special reason is required.

The following can. 985 is found in the section on the sacrament of penance: "The master of novices and his associate and the superior of a seminary or other educational institution shall not hear the sacramental confessions of their students who live in the same house with them, unless the students in particular cases freely ask that their confession be heard." This is almost the same as can. 891 of the 1917 code.

Those forbidden to act as confessors are the director or master of novices, as also the associated masters. The prohibition does not touch postulants and others, such as those of temporary vows, who may be under the master or his associates but in practice the law should be observed with regard to these also. The prohibition does not extend to those who are not properly superiors, such as deans and prefects of studies or discipline, nor does the prohibition extend to day students, but all such officials should observe the prohibition in practice also with regard to day students, since the same danger can exist in such confessions, i.e., the use of sacramental knowledge in government, the fear of a sacrilegious confession from the age of such penitents, from the respect and continuous and immediate contact with the master of novices, and from the fear of dismissal.

The confessions are forbidden in these cases "unless the students in particular cases freely ask that their confessions be heard." This excludes any restrictive or coercive means whatever, anything that could restrict the liberty of the student. The phrase "in particular cases" has commonly been understood as forbidding all habitual confessions. It is probable, however, that it can be interpreted as meaning "as long as the reason for the petition continues to exist." It can thus permit a sufficiently long series of confessions, e.g., during a time of scruples or temptations.

Some institutes have obtained privileges by which the master of novices may be the ordinary confessor of the novice. It would be at least very prudent in such cases to appoint at least another highly accessible confessor. The master may obviously never use sacramental knowledge in the government of the novices nor in his reports on the novices. I have never heard of an actual case but it would be the highest form of delusion for any confessor, no matter how holy, learned or personally attractive he may be to believe that he was also the most (or even merely) attractive to all as a confessor. The choice of a confessor in fact is usually made on subjective motives.

§ 5. *Manifestation of Conscience.* The clause on a trustful approach to superiors means only, as in can. 628, § 2, that the members are to act in a trustful manner towards their superiors. Obviously there can arise a situation in some members when in prudence they should make at least a partial manifestation to a superior. Their difficulty of conscience can be such that only a particular superior can give effective or necessary aid. All superiors in the strict sense, who are ordinarily general, provincial, and local major or minor, are forbidden to induce in any manner members, professed or novices, to make a manifestation of conscience in the strict sense, as defined below, to themselves.

Any means that takes away the free and voluntary aspects of manifestation is forbidden: 1) if done directly, e.g., by questioning on matters that fall under a manifestation; by inducing a manifestation through persuasion, promises, threats, flattery, and so forth; 2) indirectly, personally or through others by such means as praising those who make a manifestation and showing oneself averse to those who do not, by exaggerating the dangers of not making a manifestation, and so forth. Even a manifestation in the wide sense, defined below, will rarely be of much utility unless it is completely free.

Manifestation of Conscience in the Strict or Proper Sense is the revelation by a subject to a superior of his own actions that are completely interior, or, if external, are not knowable by others, provided that either is the type of action that one would not care to reveal to another except under a pledge of secrecy. Manifestation consequently includes all completely interior acts: graces, lights, good desires, inclinations, and motives; consolation, desolation; interior prayer; imperfect and evil attractions and motives; interior trials and dangers; imperfections, sins, their degree of culpability, habits of sin; and lack of effort in prayer and spiritual duties.

Manifestation only in a Wide Sense. Such matters as the knowledge of how to pray, and how to make the examination of conscience, the difficulty or ease in using particular methods of prayer or self-examination, the attraction or repugnance for particular types of spirituality, people, or occupations do not constitute a manifestation in the strict or proper sense since one would not hesitate to speak of these to another without a pledge of secrecy.

In No Sense a Manifestation of Conscience. The field of government of the religious life consists of all conduct of a member that is external and knowable to others. Superiors may legitimately question a subject about such personal conduct,and the subject is obliged to answer truthfully. See can. 628, § 1, above.

Use or Revelation of What Was Learned in a Voluntary Manifestation. No use in government whatever is permitted of what has been learned in a voluntary manifestation of conscience, without the express consent of the one who made the manifestation. It is to be presumed that the subject has given up the natural right of secrecy merely for spiritual direction, not for use. Revelation would occur when the superior would make known to a third party what he had learned in a voluntary manifestation. A manifestation constitutes an official and quasi-sacramental secret and excludes all revelation, without the express consent of the one making the manifestation.

631, § 1. *Supreme Internal Authority.* Internal authority is that possessed by religious superiors, external authority is that concerning religious and appertaining to local ordinaries. In the approval of pontifical constitutions in the past, the principle was phrased: "Supreme internal authority is exercised ordinarily by the general superior, assisted by his or her council, and extraordinarily by the legitimately assembled general chapter." In an autonomous monastery, the possessors of such authority were the superior and chapter of the monastery. There is also a council, but the monastery chapter is both an advisory body in addition to the council, and also a legislative body in constant existence.

The general chapter in centralized institutes exercises its authority rarely, usually only at the expiration of the term of the general superior. Its membership is to be so constituted that it represents the whole institute. This does not necessarily imply that every house and work will be represented in the chapter by at least one member from every house or one engaged in the particular work, e.g., when the principle of membership is to secure the most competent religious and a sufficient age diversity. The chapter will be a true sign of the unity in charity of the institute when this is its actual mode of acting. The canon lists as the principal duties of a general chapter: to protect the distinctive charism or spirit; to promote adapted renewal according to the preceding; to elect the general superior and the other elective general officials, who are at least the general councilors; to treat of the greater affairs that concern the whole institute, since the chapter does not give its attention ordinarily to particular provinces or houses; and to make enactments that all, including the general superior, must obey (see can. 578).

§ 2. *Composition and Extent of Power*. The composition of membership and the power of the chapter are to be defined in the constitutions. The latter has long been expressed, at least in lay institutes, "to treat of the more important affairs that concern the entire institute." The proper law is to determine further the order to be followed in conducting the chapter, especially concerning elections and the procedure of the treatment of affairs. Some of these, as matters of lesser moment, will be included in the directory.

§ 3. The canon declares that "provinces, local communities and also every member can freely send his requests and suggestions to the general chapter," but "according to the norms determined in proper law." I should think it a reasonable interpretation that an institute may restrict this right to those who possess active voice; otherwise those with little or no experience of the ordinary life of the institute will be forwarding many impractical proposals. The institute may also require that all proposals be handed in by a definite date, so that an apt report may be made and completed on the proposals before the chapter. The general capitulars themselves should obey this norm. However, they retain the right of making proposals during the chapter.

632. *Other Chapters and Assemblies.* In addition to the general chapter, these are provincial chapters in centralized institutes, and local, federation, and confederation chapters in institutes that have the autonomous house structure. Local chapters have not been common in centralized institutes but they now exist for the nomination or election of local superiors, councilors, other local officials, and for the approval of proposals to provincial and general chapters from the house as such. Canon 632 commands that other chapters and similar assemblies should be accurately determined in the proper law regarding their nature, authority, composition, manner of proceeding and time of celebration. However, authority is to be restricted to individual superiors and chapters, as stated in can. 501, § 1 of the preceding law and apparently in canon 596, § 1, above.

633. *Organs of Participation or Consultation.* This canon must refer to the chapters and especially "other similar assemblies," mentioned in the preceding canon, for example, provincial assemblies and enlarged councils. The present canon merely states that the members of such bodies are to perform faithfully the duties entrusted to them by law and are to be motivated by the good of the whole institute, province, region, other districts, and house. Institutes shall be wise and discreet in establishing and using such bodies, which can obviously be too numerous, make excessive demands of time and energy of their members, keep a community almost constantly agitated, and be obstructive rather than helpful to government and the good of the particular community. The canon declares finally that the manner of acting of these bodies must conform to the character and purpose of the institute.

CHAPTER III

TEMPORAL ADMINISTRATION

634. *Right of Owning Property.*

a) *Temporal Goods or Property.* These are goods, extrinsic to man, that have a value in money, e.g., money, real estate, stocks, bonds, furniture, equipment, clothing, books, and so forth. The present canon is concerned only with property owned by a religious institute, province, canonically erected house, or other public juridical person of the institute, not with that owned by individual religious. Goods of the former kind are called church or ecclesiastical property, since they are owned by a public juridical person in the Church.

b) *Capacity.* Every institute of consecrated life, province or canonically erected house is an ecclesiastical public juridical person and possesses in virtue of can. 1255 the unlimited right of acquiring, owning and administering temporal property. The same capacity for religious institutes is specified in the present can. 634, § 1, "Institutes, provinces and houses, as juridical persons by law itself, are capable of acquiring, possessing, administering and alienating temporal goods, unless this capacity is excluded or limited in the constitutions." However, can. 579 and 581 appear to state that institutes and provinces are erected by a diocesan bishop and the competent authority of the institute respectively. The latter is also affirmed of religious houses in can. 609, § 1. This language would appear to state that these religious juridical persons arise from the decree of the competent authority, not "by law itself." However, it is to be presumed that the latter is the sense of this code.

c) *Extent of Capacity.* The capacity of an institute, province or house to acquire or own property is given by canon law and is not limited by canon law. The capacity extends to all species of property, e.g., to immovable and movable goods. The former consist of things which are at least considered as being unable to be moved from place to place, e.g., lands, a church, oratory, school, hospital and so forth, and rights on such property. Movable property is that which can be so moved, e.g., clothing, furniture, equipment and so forth. The same capacity extends to all rights of use and/or receiving returns on property, e.g., interest, dividends, and rents.

d) *Exclusion or Limitation of Capacity*. The present canon, as in the past, permits the proper law of an institute to exclude or limit the proprietary capacity described above. Such limitations are practically never found in institutes of brothers or sisters; but they are found in some older institutes at least of men. Mendicant institutes are either completely or partially incapable of possessing property from which they have the right to certain and stable returns (Friars Minor, Capuchins, Discalced Carmelites and Jesuits). An institute may prescribe that the property acquired is to be spent for works and needs and that none or only a limited amount may be retained as capital. It may be enacted that the ownership of all property is vested in the institute, not in the provinces or houses or only subordinately in these. Acquisition by inheritance may be excluded absolutely or through all or some of the members.

Before adopting any such limitation an institute should make a searching investigation into its efficacy as a means of poverty and its practicality in relation to the life and work of the institute. A constant emphasis on fundamental spiritual principles and those specific to poverty can very likely be a more effective means than juridical incapacities or limitations. I have encountered practically no recent institute of simple vows that has followed any of these practices of some more ancient institutes of solemn vows. The axiom that the decline of the religious life is caused by a decline in poverty or prayer may in fact be the opposite, i.e., poverty or prayer declines because the spiritual life in general has declined.

e) *Ownership of Property*. Can. 1256 reads, "Ownership of goods belongs, under the supreme authority of the Roman Pontiff, to that juridical person which legitimately acquired the same goods." Therefore, unless otherwise specified by proper law, property is owned by the juridical person that acquired it. Houses, provinces and institutes are distinct juridical persons; therefore the assets and debts of one are not those of another. The Holy See holds the supreme administration of all church property in the sense that it is to be acquired, owned and administered according to the laws and under the authority of the Church (can. 1273). Civil incorporation is explained above under can. 609, § 1. In the canons on temporal administration, administrators of ecclesiastical property are commanded to observe canon and civil law, that the provisions of civil law on contracts are also to be observed by canon law, and that in dispositions for the good of the Church made by bequest, the solemnities of civil law should be observed whenever possible.

f) *Manner of Acquisition*. A juridical person of the religious life may acquire property, temporal goods, in any manner that is lawful to individuals according to the natural law, e.g., the fruit of one's labor, donations, purchases, inheritance, legacy, or according to the positive law of the Church or state, e.g., by contracts or wills in conformity with such laws.

g) *Property of Institute and Province*. These funds consist of the payments of novices, the interest on dowries, and the dowry itself at the death of the sister. Donations, legacies and inheritances, when given to either, also belong to the institute or province, as do the taxes on the houses for the general and provincial government, of the novitiate, juniorate, education and formation of the members, central infirmary, the erection of houses, the assistance of the poorer works and houses, and, if possible, the establishment of a reserve fund for extraordinary expenses, and of a capital fund that will serve as a source of regular income for some or all of these purposes.

h) *General and Provincial Tax*. The general and provincial expenses are clearly necessary. They are for the good of the entire institute or province and must, at least in very great part, be defrayed by contributions from the provinces and houses. Two species of taxation were found in constitutions:

One-third of the Net Surplus of the Past Year. According to the *Normae* of 1901, no. 294, each house was obliged to send this sum at the end of each year to the provincial or general treasury, if there were no provinces, and each province had to send the same fraction of its net surplus to the general treasury. The tax should be sufficient to take care of the general and provincial expenses; it should not burden all or some of the provinces and houses excessively nor prevent the establishments of the institute from setting up a reserve fund for proper maintenance and development. An obvious defect of this system is that it is only a contingent payment. It depends on the fact of a surplus. The general and provincial expenses are absolute and constant; the tax should therefore be an absolute element of the house and provincial budgets. It should be condoned or lessened when a province or house simply cannot pay it.

Determined Sum for Each Member. A more modern and preferable norm found in many constitutions approved more recently by the Holy See is that the determination of the amount of the tax is left to the general chapter or superior. It can then be increased or decreased as the times and circumstances demand. The chapter or superior has often determined that each house is to contribute a fixed sum annually for each member assigned to the work of the house. A fractional part of such a sum may then be assigned to the general funds when the institute is divided into provinces, or each province may be assessed a flat sum according to its resources. The amount fixed by the constitutions or the general chapter is the minimum contribution; no house or province is forbidden freely to give more within the limits of ordinary administration.

i) *Extraordinary Tax.* If the ordinary tax does not suffice, the general superior, with the consent of the council, may impose an extraordinary tax on the provinces and houses. He may in like manner authorize or confirm an extraordinary tax on the houses of a province requested or made by the provincial superior, with the deliberative vote of his council. The parts of an institute are obliged to work for the common good and thus to contribute also to extraordinary expenses. The general chapter or the proper law of an institute may grant the authority to the general and provincial superiors to impose such a tax and to increase or decrease the ordinary tax.

j) *Salaries in Institutions That Belong to Others*. A special case is verified in houses or works that are owned by others and in which the income of the religious community consists of salaries paid for the members by the proprietors or administrators of such works, e.g., parish schools, diocesan high schools, orphanages, hospitals, and other institutions owned by the diocese, a private secular corporation, the city or the state. Such communities are obliged to give all their surplus to the provincial or general funds, i.e., all that is not necessary for the support of the members of the particular community. They are to retain above this only what is permitted by the general chapter or higher superiors. This norm is occasionally contained explicitly in the constitutions. Its reasonableness is clear from the fact that such a community has no financial liability for its own residence or the institutions and consequently no need of surplus funds.

k) *Other Contributions from Provinces and Houses. Salaries and Gifts*. Anything whatever acquired by a solemnly professed and by any religious at least for his work, with respect to his institute, or as a pension, assistance or insurance (can. 668, § 3) belongs to his institute. The constitutions or directory may determine whether the proprietorship of such acquisitions appertains wholly or partially to the houses, provinces, or institute. The constitutions have almost always been silent on this point, and the determination may then be made by the general chapter or higher superiors. The same principle extends to purely personal gifts made to members and turned in by them, and the determination may be made by the same authorities as in the preceding case. This is also true when a gift has been clearly made to a member for his institute but the donor has in no way determined the part of the institute to which the gift is to go.

l) *Transfer of Property From One Part of an Institute to Another*. According to Vatican II, "Provinces and houses of a religious institute should share their resources with one another, those which are better supplied assisting those which suffer need" (PC, no. 13). The principle certainly confirms the probable doctrine of the past that property may be transferred from one part of an institute to another when the latter is in need. The general chapter or major superiors are the competent authorities for permitting such a transfer from one house or province to another or to the provincial or general funds, e.g., if one house is in great material need or for the transfer of valuable books that are useless in one house to another where they are needed.

   m) *Inventories*. Both good administration and the general can. 1283 demand that each institute, province and house maintain an inventory of all property that belongs to it. This practice is also and especially to be observed in establishments owned by others, e.g., in parish convents an inventory is to be kept of all property owned by the religious community. A brief description and at least the approximate value of each object is to be noted in the inventory. The inventory is to be kept up-to-date and should therefore be revised at reasonable intervals. A copy of the inventory of a house is to be kept also in the files of the province or institute.

634, § 2; 635, § 2. *Proper Laws on Poverty*. The first canon commands the avoidance of even the appearance of luxury, excessive gain or profit or accumulation of goods. This accumulation is not verified in a reasonable reserve fund or capital funds to assist in such ends as formation and the care of the incapacitated and aged, secondary schools, colleges, universities, nursing homes, other homes for the aged, and other works of the institute. Such funds are characterized among religious evidently much more by their absence than their excess. According to the prescript of can. 635, § 2, each religious institute should enact suitable norms on the use and administration of goods that will express, promote and protect its proper poverty.

635, § 1. *Norm of Religious Institutes Concerning Temporal Goods*. The law that regulates religious institutes in this matter is the section of the canons on ecclesiastical goods or property, which is the universal law of the Church. It is evident, however, that added norms are established for religious institutes in this chapter on the temporal goods of religious institutes.

636, § 1. *Necessity of Treasurers*. Major superiors, namely the general and provincial superiors, as well as those of autonomous houses, and also minor superiors of canonically erected houses are obliged by this canon to have a treasurer. The latter are to work under the authority of the superiors. Consequently both the government of persons and the administration of property are under the authority of superiors. The local treasurer is to be distinct, as far as possible, from the minor local superior; the treasurer is to be distinct from both the general and provincial superior.

Duties. The respective superior may act directly with regard to temporal matters but he should do so only in special cases, e.g., to supply for the absence, deficiencies or remissness of the treasurer. The direct and immediate administration is ordinarily left to the treasurer. It appertains to the particular directory, customs, or appointment of superiors to determine whether the office is purely that of treasurer or whether it extends to the care of all ordinary temporal matters, e.g., of the necessities of all in food, clothing, the material condition and maintenance of the house and its furnishings. Major superiors may appoint an administrator for a particular matter, e.g., the securing of funds for the erection of a building. They may likewise appoint someone to audit the books and examine the entire administration of treasurers. In many institutes it would be more practical to assign this duty ordinarily to the general and provincial treasurers.

§ 2. *Financial Reports*. The general norm of frequency of reports by ecclesiastical administrators is once a year (can. 1284, § 2). It has been the practically universal norm in constitutions approved by the Holy See, at least of lay institutes, that the accounts of the general and provincial treasurers are examined every six months and those of a local treasurer monthly by the respective superiors and their councils. The examination would be facilitated and be more accurate if copies were made for all the councilors and distributed to them sufficiently before the session. The financial statements should be so itemized and accompanied by written explanations that all can readily understand the complete state of the general and provincial funds and the financial condition of the local house. The general and provincial councils have had a deliberative vote in the approval of accounts.

Reports From Provinces and Houses. In the same practice, every six months a statement of the financial condition of a province and all its houses was sent by the provincial to the general superior and by the local to provincial superiors or, when there were no provinces, to the general superior. These norms varied only rarely, e.g., the report from the provinces in some institutes was every year or every three months and that of the local superiors was forwarded each month. The constitutions stated merely that these reports were to be sent to the higher superior. Not all, therefore, explicitly prescribed that they be presented to the general and provincial councils, but these should evidently be kept informed of the material state of the institute and province. From these reports, the treasurer should prepare a statement that will enable the respective superior to see readily the financial state of the institute or province. The laudable practice has been introduced into several institutes of presenting, at least annually and to all its members, a financial statement of the house, province and institute.

637. *Financial Reports to the Local Ordinary.* The autonomous monasteries of nuns mentioned in can. 615 must render an account of administration once a year to the local ordinary, who determines the form of the account. This ordinary also has the right of knowing the financial accounts of a diocesan religious house of men or women. The manner, time and frequency of the latter are left to his determination. In this latter case, the ordinary is given the right, not commanded to exact such knowledge, nor is his right extended to the institute as such.

638, § 1. *Determination of Acts That Exceed Ordinary Administration.* In the past there was agreement on the concept of temporal administration in general, i.e., that it consisted of all acts by which property, or temporal goods, already acquired was conserved, maintained in condition for its purpose, improved, made more useful or productive, by which returns on property were secured, e.g., interests and rents, and the property and its fruits applied to their proper purposes, e.g., the works of the institute or the sustenance of its members. The point of the present canon is that the acts that are to be classified as extraordinary administration are to be determined in the proper law of each religious institute. Requisites for the valid, and a fortiori for the licit, execution of an act of extraordinary administration may be enacted in proper law.

Examples of *ordinary administration* as conceived in the past were: the buying of things required for the daily necessities of the community; the depositing of money in banks for facility in handling , for security, and to obtain some interest; the receipt of income such as tuitions, salaries, payment of debts, interest, rents, fees from patients in hospitals and other institutions; to make and receive gifts of lesser moment; and to make ordinary repairs and renovations.

Examples of *extraordinary administration* were: the acceptance or refusal, in the name of the juridical person, of an inheritance, a legacy, or a gift made with the formalities of civil law; the purchase of immovable property; the contracting of a loan of money that could burden or endanger the stable patrimony of the juridical person; making of extraordinary repairs and renovations; erecting a building; taking part in a lawsuit concerning temporal goods; investing of money or the changing of an investment; exchanging of stocks and bonds; alienation of property; mortgaging of property, putting up property as security for a debt; extraordinary gifts and expenses; and extraordinary repairs and renovations.

Most of the items listed above caused no problem. The obscurity was found in the prominently practical matters of extraordinary purchases, expenses, repairs, renovations that were concretely replacements of existing equipment such as a new community car or refrigerator, and extraordinary gifts or alms. It was not too difficult to admit that the replacement of a car or refrigerator was an ordinary expense because it was a replacement. Did this argument apply also to the replacement of heating furnaces in a large building or complex of buildings? Different norms may be established for different types of work, e.g., one for smaller establishments and one for larger, especially those that use a great quantity and variety of equipment, as is true of hospitals.

The more usual practice under the present heading was to fix a certain money level as the determinant of extraordinary administration, e.g., the cost of a purchase. The determination was left to the general chapter, which could then vary the determined sum as the times demanded. The usual practice also was to fix a sum that local superiors could spend for extraordinary expenses of all kinds. For anything beyond that they had to recur to higher superiors for permission. The greater sum that provincial and general superiors could spend or authorize was also determined. On all these levels the consultative or deliberative vote of the respective council could be demanded or prescribed only for the higher sum on each level of authority. The vote of the council was commonly deliberative.

§ 2. *Competency for Ordinary Administration*. Superiors, treasurers and other officials designated in proper law are competent to place acts of ordinary administration in virtue of their office. The proper law, general chapter or regulation of higher superiors may demand the permission of a higher authority for the liceity or even the validity of more serious acts of ordinary administration.

Depositing and Investment of Money. Depositing of money in a bank for greater security, more efficient administration, or to obtain some interest is not considered in canon law as an investment. Therefore, when money either strictly or morally remains in the possession of the owner so that it can be recovered again either immediately or after a brief interval, the act is not an investment and falls under ordinary administration. Investment of money is the at least relatively permanent conversion of money into other productive property, e.g., into real estate to be leased or into stocks and bonds. Prudence demands that the permission of at least the immediate higher superior should be required for an investment, which could be given habitually for a particular type of investment. Prudence also urges that investments should be made only after consultation with an honest and competent financier. A list of the investments and their current market value should be part of the report made to the superior and his council and to major superiors.

§ 3. *Alienation, Precious Objects, Debts, Obligations*. The basic
ideas of alienation are given in the universal law of can. 1291, " . . . to
alienate goods which have been legitimately designated as the stable
patrimony of a public juridical person," and in can. 1295, "for alienation but also for any transaction by which the patrimonial state of a
juridical person could become less favorable." Alienation may therefore
be defined as *the transferring to another, wholly or partially, or the
endangering of the ownership of property appertaining to the stable
patrimony of a juridical person*. 1) *Another*. This other must be a
completely distinct physical or juridical person, e.g., the sale of land to a
business corporation. Because of the close moral union that exists among
them, it is solidly probable that the canonical norms for alienation and
the contracting of debts and obligations do not apply to such transactions
between houses, provinces, and the institute itself. 2) *Transferring*. a)
Expropriation. Alienation is a contract, a voluntary act. Therefore,
expropriation, or the sale of property forced by a government is not
considered canonically as alienation. b) *Transferring*. This is verified by
such acts as giving away, selling, or exchanging. c) *Wholly*. For example, the selling of land or of a house is alienation. d) *Partially*. For
example, to grant another a partial right on the lands of a religious house
is alienation. Since only the form of the property is changed and the
assets are not diminished, it is not alienation to use the funds of stable
capital to repair buildings; to purchase or erect residence buildings for
the members, especially if these would otherwise have to be rented; or to
purchase or erect buildings that will yield income (schools, hospitals,
and so forth). It is alienation to use such funds to improve buildings. For
the same reason, it is not alienation but a change of investment to
exchange stocks and bonds for other stocks and bonds that are at least
equally secure and productive or to change them into the simple placing
of money at interest, or into an investment in productive real estate.

For the same reason, it is not alienation to give a loan with or without
interest but with adequate security; to sell old furnishings to buy new
furnishings; and to sell that which is rather a cause of loss than of utility
or profit, e.g., to sell a house that is in ruins and to sell fields that are

producing little or no profit if the expense of cultivating them or of making them profitable would be very great. e) *Endangering*. This consists of acts that expose the juridical person to the danger of losing property, e.g., the mortgaging of a determined property and making property the surety or guarantee for the payment of the debt or obligation of another. f) *Ownership of Property—of a Juridical Person*. Alienation affects either immovable or movable property actually owned by a public juridical person. Therefore, alienation does not apply to property owned by individual members. It is not alienation to repudiate a profit, inheritance, or legacy, because these acts are the refusal to acquire property. Neither is it alienation to erect a building and place a mortgage on the building at the time of the erection, or to purchase a building or land previously burdened with a mortgage and to assume this mortgage, since these are considered canonically as less perfect acquisitions of property. g) *Appertaining to the Stable Patrimony*. Stable patrimony is that portion of the juridical person's property that is removed from ordinary circulation and constitutes the permanent basis of its financial security. Immovable property, e.g., a house or lands, by its nature appertains to stable patrimony. Immovable property can be equivalently free capital, e.g., it is not alienation to sell such property when it has been given or bequeathed to a juridical person with the explicit or implicit intention that it be sold and used for such a purpose as the sustenance of its members, their formation or their works. Precious objects are part of stable patrimony, as is movable and non-perishable and perishable property taken collectively. Money does not appertain to this patrimony unless it has been legitimately set aside by competent authority as a permanent source of regularly accruing income.

Perishable goods, if considered non-collectively, of their nature do not constitute stable patrimony. Therefore, it is not alienation to give away fruit, grain, eggs, a cow or sheep, but it is alienation to transfer the proprietorship of an entire herd of cows or an entire flock of sheep. The same distinction applies to movable and non-perishable goods. It is not alienation to sell or give away a few books, a desk, a chair, but it is alienation to do this with regard to a library, all the furnishings of a house, and so forth.

To expend money from free capital or a reserve fund is not alienation. Free capital consists of the funds destined for the regularly recurring expenses; reserve funds are those set aside for future needs. The only money that can be alienated canonically is that appertaining to stable patrimony, which was defined above. Therefore, it is not alienation to meet ordinary or extraordinary expenses to pay a debt, purchase real estate, or erect buildings from current or reserve funds. It is not alienation to place money in safe investments, e.g., stocks, bonds, and the like, until favorable opportunities or sufficient sums warrant the construction of buildings, because this money had not been set aside as stable capital.

Precious Objects. These are defined as precious in can. 638, § 3 because of artistic reasons, e.g., statues, tapestries, paintings, ornamented vases, or for historical reasons, such as codices, old coins, first editions, and public or private documents. Objects precious because of their material are no longer included in the definition and are therefore governed by the common norms on alienation. Merely because they are precious, such objects cannot be validly alienated without the permission of the Holy See. The phrase "of notable value" of the 1917 code has been omitted.

Debts. These are not explicitly mentioned with alienation, as in the 1917 code. *A debt is a contractual obligation to repay, with or without interest, a specified sum of money.* The canonical norms on alienation extend to debts only insofar as the latter are in fact alienations, i.e., those debts that burden the stable patrimony of a juridical person. A debt here is first a long term debt. Short term loans, e.g., debts that can certainly be paid from the normal revenues of the house, province or institute within a brief period, such as two years, are not long term debts. The essential reason, however, is that they do not burden the stable patrimony.

A *secured loan* is a debt in the canonical sense to the extent that the collateral security appertains to stable capital, not when it is entirely from free capital or reserve funds. An *unsecured promissory note* and a loan obtained on general credit constitute a debt in the canonical sense if and to the extent that stable patrimony could be seized for their payment; in other words, when the free capital and reserve funds are not completely sufficient for their payment. Proper permission should be secured for all non-canonical debts according to any enactments of the general chapter or instructions of higher superiors. Obviously any other transaction, whatever be its name, that objectively verifies the concept of alienation falls under the norms for the latter (can. 1295).

Antecedent Requisites for Permission to Alienate. Mention must be made of parts previously alienated of a divisible object, e.g., of land or a library; otherwise the permission obtained is invalid (can. 1292, § 3). Advice or consent should not be given by anyone to an alienation unless he has been previously informed in detail about the economic condition and prior alienations of the juridical person whose goods are to be alienated (can. 1292, § 4). Alienation also requires (can. 1293, § 1, 1°): a just cause, such as urgent necessity, evident usefulness, piety, charity, pastoral good; a written estimate by experts of the goods to be alienated; other precautions prescribed by a legitimate authority should be observed to prevent loss to the Church.

In and After the Alienation. (can. 1294). Ordinarily an object should not be alienated for a price less than its estimated value. The money realized from alienation should be wisely invested for the good of the Church or prudently spent in accord with the purposes of the alienation.

Requisite Permission for Religious Institutes (can. 638, § 3). The permission of the Holy See is required for the validity of an alienation: if the particular goods had been donated to the Church in accord with a vow; if they are precious objects; or if the value of the particular goods exceeds the amount established by the Holy See for the region. The superior competent for lesser sums must have the written consent of his or her local ordinary in an autonomous monastery of can. 615 or a diocesan institute (638, § 4).

Proper Law. The proper law of an institute should certainly require the written permission (see can. 638, § 1) of the general superior, with the consent of his council, for a request to the Holy See for alienation. The superior, also with the consent of his council, competent to grant written permission for lesser amounts will depend on the amounts established by the Holy See for the various regions in which the institute has houses. This amount may vary in value for various episcopal conferences, even in countries of the same economic level, and it can also be changed. It might be better to leave the determination of the authority competent for lesser sums, below that requiring the permission of the Holy See, to general chapter enactments rather than to include it in the constitutions or even in the directory.

639. *Responsibility for Debts and Obligations.* § 1. If a religious juridical person, i.e., a house, province or institute has contracted debts or obligations with or without the permission of a higher superior or authority, such as the Holy See or a local ordinary, the contracting juridical person is solely responsible. The permission makes the contract licit but is not a guarantee of the debt, which is a matter of further express provision or agreement. § 2. If a member, with the permission of his superior, made a contract regarding his own goods, he is responsible; but if, with the mandate or commission of the superior, he carried out a business affair of the institute, the institute (institute, province, or house) is responsible. § 3. If a religious contracted without any permission of superiors, he is responsible, not the juridical person. § 4. In any case, whether the juridical person or an individual religious is responsible, the one suffering loss by the contract may institute an action against any individual or any juridical person if and to the extent that either has profited by the contract. § 5. *Caution in Granting Permission to Contract Debts.* Religious superiors are to take care not to allow debts to be contracted unless they are certain that the religious juridical person can pay the interest from its ordinary and regular, not exceptional and unusual, income and that the capital debt can be paid off within a period that is not too long.

640. *Gifts and the Giving of Alms by Institutes.* Following Vatican II, this canon enacts: ''Institutes, consideration being had for the individual

places, should strive to render a quasi-collective testimony of charity and poverty, and as far as possible give some contribution from their goods to necessities of the Church and for the sustenance of the needy." Can. 1285, on church possessions, states: "Within the limits of ordinary administration it is permissible for administrators of movable goods which do not pertain to a stable patrimony to make donations for piety or christian charity."

The reference in both of these canons is to alms and gifts from religious houses, provinces, and institutes. The norm will often consist of a specified sum that each superior is permitted to give away annually. He will be required to ask permission of a higher superior for gifts beyond that sum. The motive of gifts or alms will frequently be gifts to benefactors, the obtaining of good will for the institute or its works, gifts to the poor, to hospitals, and to institutions for the diseased, aged, or unfortunate. Charity should be shown first by gifts to the houses, works, and members of the same institute, such as those for the support, education, and formation of the novices and young professed members, for the missions and needy houses of the institute, and for the needy relatives of members of the institute.

Duties to Employees. According to can. 1286 on church property: "Administrators of goods: 1° In hiring employees should diligently obey civil laws that regulate labor relations and social life, in accord with the principles handed down by the Church; 2° Should pay to those who work by contract a just and honest salary so that they and their families will be able to provide properly for their own and the necessities of their dependents."

Collection of Offerings. Canon 1265, § 2 on church property, declares, "A conference of bishops may establish regulations governing the solicitation of offerings, which should be observed by all, not excluding those who from their foundation are called and are mendicant." The norms for the United States, approved by the National Conference of Catholic Bishops, November 14-17, 1977, are found in O'Connor, *Canon Law Digest,* vol. 8, pp. 415 ff., and in summary form in RfR, 40 (1981), pp. 103-5, which read as follows.

Christian Stewardship. Stewardship is a practical realization that everything we have is a gift from God. We are absolute owners of nothing, but stewards of all we receive. Stewardship heightens an awareness of responsibilities in matters of material concern no less than in spiritual endeavor. This is especially true when we, in God's name and for his work, ask others for financial support. A fitting proportion must be had between the importance of the work to be funded and the magnitude and cost of fund raising. Requests for support must be truthful and forthright, made on a theologically sound basis, and always in good taste.

Stewardship Guidelines. No organization should ask the faithful to fund its total and absolute security nor for undefined future needs. The trust between donor and fund raiser requires that funds collected be used for the intended purpose and not be absorbed by excessive fund-raising costs. Restrictions stated by the donor must be observed.

Religious Authority. All who collect funds under Catholic auspices must have the clear and explicit approval of appropriate Church authority.

Religious Authority Guidelines. Religious institutes and diocesan agencies should observe canonical prescriptions and their own regulations which require the approval of major superiors and/or the ordinary of the place to solicit funds. The approval by proper authority should express the purpose for which the funds are raised and the methods to be used in raising them. Effective control of fund-raising programs should be maintained through periodic review and, where necessary, appropriate sanctions. Religious or diocesan agencies may not collect funds by public subscription without the consent of the ordinaries of the places where the funds are collected. Major superiors of religious institutes should as a moral duty provide the ordinary of the places where the fund raising originates with significant information about the fund raising programs and the apostolates they support.

Accountability and Guidelines. The fund raiser must recognize that giving as an expression of religion has a sacramental nature. Fund raisers are accountable to the donor for the disposition of monies received. This accountability demands that funds be used for the causes promoted and respect always for the specified wishes of the donor. Furthermore, fund raisers should make available to donors an appropriate report of significant financial aspects, and the apostolic dimensions of the endeavor to which they have contributed. Fund raisers are to provide timely reports, which should be prepared to meet the particular concerns of those to whom reports are due: namely, the governing body and membership of the fund-raising organization, religious authorities who approved and must monitor the fund-raising effort, donors to the particular organization, the giving public at large, and those who are beneficiaries of the funds given.

Fund-raising reports should provide financial information and a review of the apostolic work for which the funds were raised. The availability of these reports to benefactors on a regular basis or on reasonable request should be publicized. Fund-raising organizations should provide their governing bodies with an annual audit prepared in accordance with generally accepted accounting principles and, where size warrants, by a certified public accountant. All financial reports of a fund raiser should be consistent with the annual audit. A fund raiser's report should set forth at least the amount of money collected, the cost of conducting the fund raising, and the amount and use of the funds disbursed. Donations should be acknowledged with promptness. Reasonable requests from donors for information about their particular gifts should be met.

Technique. Exclusive authority over all aspects of fund raising should not be vested in any single person. Separation of such financial functions of fund raising as collection, allocation and accounting is essential for internal control. Adherence to legal requirements and respect for professional guidelines are fundamental to sound management of fund raising. Responsible and effective fund-raising methodology should never drown out the voice of the Spirit of God that must permeate our total efforts.

Technique Guidelines. Funds beyond operating expenses should not be accumulated by a fund-raising office but should be turned over at regular intervals to the appropriate allocating office. Fund-raising authority and investment authority should not be vested in any single person. Special care should be taken that ethical business relationships are maintained by fund raisers with suppliers of goods and services. Contracts between a religious fund raiser and commercial suppliers and consultants should insure that control over materials, designs, money and general operations remains fully in the hands of the religious fund raiser. Agreements should never be made that directly or indirectly base payment either to the commercial firm or to the religious fund raiser on a percentage basis. Requests for funds should not be associated with material objects inconsistent with the apostolic purpose of the appeal.

Implementation Guidelines. Local ordinaries and major superiors should exercise control over fund-raising activities to achieve conformity with these guidelines. Legitimate authority, especially in response to formal complaints, should promptly investigate charges and remedy abuses, even to the point, when necessary, of terminating a fund-raising program.

In virtue of their endorsement of these guidelines, the NCCB, the LCWR, and CMSM agree to assist their members in achieving appropriate control of fund-raising activities and in obtaining effective sanction for abuses. Each conference through its president will: a) promulgate these guidelines and other suitable norms for responsible fund raising; b) help correct abuses through cooperative efforts with the responsible authorities and a meeting of the presidents of these three conferences to collaborate on further action, if an abuse on the part of a member not be resolved by that member's responsible authority (CLD, 8, pp. 415-21).

CHAPTER IV

ADMISSION OF CANDIDATES AND FORMATION OF MEMBERS

641. *Competent Major Superior for Admission into the Noviceship*. Admission into an institute is identical with admission into the noviceship. The canons do not contain a postulancy. Admission into the noviceship is the juridical act of the higher superior, competent according to the constitutions, and previous to the actual entrance of the candidate, by which he decides that a candidate may enter the institute as a novice. It seems to me that all acts of admission, e.g., admission to the first profession, renewals, prolongations, final profession, as also receptions of professions and exclusions from them of their nature appertain to higher superiors. An admission is not merely to a house but to a province and an institute. As such it transcends the level of mere local government.

Furthermore, one would argue a fortiori from the present canon that all other admissions, e.g., to first profession, appertain also to a major superior. The competent higher superior here is the general superior, but in institutes divided into provinces he would normally be the provincial superior, and in autonomous monasteries and houses the local major superior. According to the past practice, the general and provincial superior admitted into the noviceship with the deliberative vote of the respective council. In some institutes, admission by the provincial required also the consent of the general superior alone or with the deliberative or consultative vote of his council. In autonomous monasteries, the local major superior admitted with the deliberative vote of the chapter.

The canon itself does not require any vote of a council or chapter; obviously it permits that a vote be consultative or deliberative. Can. 597, § 2 demands an appropriate pre-entrance preparation, and § 1 that those admitted be Catholics.

642. *Necessary Suitability. Divine Vocation.* The fundamental element in a vocation to the clerical or religious life is the special call, election or choice by God, which more recent documents of the Holy See style as a divine vocation. In his Apostolic Constitution of May 31, 1956, *Sedes Sapientiae*, Pius XII stated:

"First we would have everyone remember that the foundation of the religious and of the sacerdotal and apostolic life, which is called a divine vocation, consists of two essential elements, one divine, the other ecclesiastical. As to the first of these, a call from God to enter the religious life or the sacerdotal state is so necessary that if this is lacking, the very foundations on which the whole edifice rests is wanting (C 12).

"And this not only does not contradict what we said about a divine vocation, but is strictly consistent with it, since it destines a man to lead publicly a life of sanctification and to exercise the hierarchical ministry in the Church, that is, in a visible and hierarchical society, it has to be authoritatively approved, admitted, and controlled also by hierarchical superiors, to whom the government of the Church has been divinely entrusted" (C 15).

The choice, election or call of God is communicated to a person through grace, the illumination and inspiration of the Holy Spirit, and ordinarily at least in a series of acts, which culminate in the decisive and supernatural intention to become a religious. The supernatural, or graced, aspect of the intention is deduced and ascertained primarily from the rectitude of the motives.

1) *Intention.* An intention is the will do something. The object of the intention in this case is to be a member of a religious institute. Therefore, the primary explicit or implicit motive of the candidate must be to strive for the perfection of charity through the observance of the evangelical counsels, the life, and the constitutions of the particular institute. This motive may be implicit. An aspirant who wishes to be more perfectly

conformed to Christ, to serve God more perfectly, to secure the greater spiritual aids of the religious life is implicitly intending the religious life. It is not required that the candidate have theologically analyzed his intention. If an aspirant has been educated in the school of a religious institute or is familiar with its life from other external observation or sources and wishes to dedicate himself to this same life, he has the proper motive in the concrete in his intention.

On the other hand, a motive that is solely or primarily human and natural is not sufficient for a vocation to the religious life. The aspirant then is not to be admitted until the human motive is excluded or at least made subordinate to the true supernatural motive. Such motives can and do occur, e.g., the desire of a life of honor and ease, freedom from responsibility, escape from personal or family problems, material security, mere friendship for a member of the institute, the fact that a brother or sister has entered, and a greater opportunity for study. Some motives of this nature, e.g., that of friendship, can be the occasion from which a true vocation arises (see can. 597, § 1).

The intention considered in its source is the human will aided by the grace of the Holy Spirit. An intention of the following type in which grace acts more on the will than the mind, is sufficient but not necessary. There is relatively little reflection, the person almost instinctively realizes that the religious life is the only life for him, almost instinctively also is imbued with a strong attachment to the religious life, is filled with sensible consolation at the thought of entering this state and with corresponding repugnance at remaining in secular life. In the ordinary intention grace acts more on the intellect by assisting the Christian to see what is pleasing to God rather than on the will by sensible inclinations and consolation. The individual sees that the religious life is preferable for him and wills to enter it.

These two types of intention are not always sharply divided. There must be sufficient reflection in the first, and there can be some measure of consolation in the latter. The second type especially is compatible with some repugnance to the religious life or to certain of its aspects. This is true of an ordinary act of virtue and is even more likely in the intention to enter the religious life. It is not reasonable to expect that a life of complete self-renunciation should be wholly attractive to the pride and sensuality of fallen human nature. Whether or not the repugnance is of such a nature or so intense as to preclude perseverance is something that depends on a prudent judgment of the particular case.

The intention of becoming a member should also be firm and constant. This is to be ascertained from the length of time that the aspirant has had such an intention, from the seriousness of the consideration given to it, and from its source. Has the aspirant had the thought and intention only in moments of fervor, exaltation, of agitation, trouble, anxiety, when confronted by problems of secular life, or has he considered it at times of calm of soul, in prayer, and when one is quietly united with God?

2) *Negative Aptitude*. A religious vocation is certainly lacking when the candidate does not possess aptitude for the life of the institute. The grace of the Holy Spirit does not invite to the religious life one who is unfit for that life. Much of the unhappiness and problems in the religious life is caused not only by those culpably unfaithful to it but also by those incapable for it. Negative aptitude consists in freedom from the impediments of canon law and of the constitutions of the particular institute. These impediments will be explained under can. 643. Negative aptitude is not lacking if the impediment is dispensable and the admitting higher superior has a sufficient reason for securing a dispensation and intends to do so. Higher superiors are obviously to make sure that the applicant possesses negative aptitude but they are not to exaggerate its importance. Negative aptitude proves very little with regard to the suitability of the candidate. What do you know about him from the fact that he has proved certainly that he is seventeen years of age? Positive aptitude is of much greater practical importance.

3) *Positive Aptitude*. The applicant must have the ability to live creditably the religious life and that of the particular institute. This demands sufficient physical and mental health, suitable habits of mind and will, and at least satisfactory ability for the life and works of the particular institute.

a) *Physical Health*. The applicant should have sufficient physical health for the life and work of the particular institute. He should be required to undergo a general physical examination by a doctor carefully chosen by the institute. Such doctors can be familiarized with the physical demands of the institute. He should fill out a common form for each candidate, which should also contain space for any special observations and for his own conclusion. Experience has demonstrated the inefficiency of the practice of permitting the applicant to choose his own doctor for the examination.

b) *Mental Health*. Some institutes use a form of psychological testing for screening their candidates. No one can deny the need of much greater care under this heading. The very odd professed were usually also very odd candidates. Pronounced nervousness and tenseness, constant and serious scrupulosity, and a lack of common sense and good judgment are among the personality defects that make one unsuitable for the religious life. The greatest deficiency has been the failure to perceive and study the odd, peculiar, queer, moody, melancholy, taciturn and unsocial characters.

To decide whether the greater maturity, the education, formation, and counseling of the institute will enable the individual to overcome such traits satisfactorily and that he may be given the trial of the noviceship will often require most serious consideration. An apt pre-entrance period of preparation will be an aid to such a judgment. Immaturity is a word heard constantly under this heading. The candidate should have the maturity required to accept the grace of a vocation responsibly, to make a very profitable noviceship, and to be ready for first profession at the normal time of one or two years. A long probation is not necessarily maturing nor does it necessarily detect the immature. All of these facts prove that the immediate higher superior should maintain close contact with the novitiate and should receive frequent reports from the directors of candidates and novices.

New Provision in Can. 642. The canon reaffirms recourse to specialists, if this is necessary to establish the health, character and sufficient maturity of candidates but it also adds a reference to can. 220,

"No one is permitted . . . to violate the right of every person of protecting his own innermost privacy," which is my translation of the Latin original, "intimitas."

Psychological interviews, examinations and testing have been an added means in wide use to evaluate and establish the psychological fitness of candidates. They are a supplement to the traditional methods of direct observation, personal interviews, and the seeking of information from responsible individuals. The vigorous added requirement concerning personal privacy leads us to hold that a candidate must be previously informed of the nature of the tests, of their purpose of discerning his psychological fitness, that they can reveal even disqualifying psychological disorders, that his voluntary consent be given to undergo them as also that the results be communicated to the one in charge of admissions. Personal privacy is certainly primarily psychic privacy.

3) *Suitable Habits of Mind and Will.* These should be such as constitute at least credible aptitude for an outstanding religious life. The religious life is not for the mediocre. A candidate will rarely be so attached to luxuries and his own comfort or so tenacious of judgment and stubborn of will that he cannot be given at least the trial of the noviceship. Poverty and obedience therefore do not ordinarily cause difficulties against admission. The same principle is true of defects contrary to common life, such as an unrestrained temper and habit of gossip. However, aptitude for a community social life is by no means to be passed over.

Chastity can be a practical problem, but the judgment in this matter almost always appertains to the confessor. It should be morally certain at the time of first profession that the novice, with the grace of God, will be able to live a life of perfect chastity. Negatively this implies that any evil habits of the past have been completely overcome and that no future lapse can be foreseen because of such habits. The confessor, especially in the case of solitary sin, should form his judgment from many factors. He should demand a period of trial of at least six months of complete victory, the result of which has been a quiet assurance of conquest and not a continuous strained effort. The confessor is also to consider whether his penitent is studious, zealous, industrious, and otherwise spiritually inclined. He must study the source of the habit and learn whether it comes from an extrinsic source such as careless reading or immodesty of the senses or from the more difficult source of a character defect, when the penitent can be seeking relief or escape from nervousness, depression or an unsociable nature.

If the habit returns after first profession and is not perfectly overcome, the religious may not be permitted to renew temporary vows or to make perpetual profession. Greater care and strictness are evidently to be exercised at the time of perpetual profession. Some authors demand for one entering the religious life only a founded hope of attaining perfect chastity by the time of his first profession, but it would be at least far more prudent to require this chastity also at the time of entrance into a religious institute. An added reason for this principle is that the constant problem of daily communion faces the novice also. It is the common teaching of authors that experience counsels greater severity rather than lenience in the entire matter of the aptitude for a life of perfect chastity.

4) *Satisfactory Ability for the Works of the Institute.* The works of an institute are partially the purpose of its existence and must obviously also be the norm for the admission of candidates. No candidate should be admitted unless there is at least serious probability that he can be educated and formed satisfactorily for some works of the institute. Other things being equal, encouragement and preference are to be given to the more capable. In those whose capacity is doubtful, compensating gifts are not to be presumed but proved. The fact that an occasional religious of lesser ability has accomplished great things cannot logically or sanely be applied to every candidate of lesser ability. These evident principles are often forgotten.

5) *Refusal of a Vocation.* Since the religious life is of counsel, it is not in itself a sin to refuse to follow the grace of a vocation. It is possible for an obligation of entering the religious life to exist from such extrinsic sources as a vow of becoming a member or from the certainty that God has commanded the individual person to enter. It is evident that such an obligation, especially the latter, is most rarely verified in fact. It is not

true that the refusal to accept a vocation is sinful because it necessarily exposes the person to eternal damnation by remaining in secular life. God will not give such a person the graces that he would have received to live a holy religious life but he will receive sufficient and, if he prays, efficacious graces for a secular life, whose purpose is also a life of sanctity.

The principles given above are also true of the freedom of a novice to leave at any time during the noviceship and of a professed of temporary vows to leave at the expiration of any temporary profession. No law of the Church obliges these to remain. The novice has not as yet assumed the obligation of vows, and such an obligation has expired for the professed of temporary vows. No law of God obliges them to remain, since the principles given above for the refusal to accept a vocation apply equally to these cases.

643, § 1. *Canonical and Diriment Impediments to Entrance into the Noviceship.* The first sentence of the canon states that one bound by any of these impediments is invalidly admitted to the noviceship, but the sense is clearly, as in the 1917 code, that one bound by any of these impediments invalidly enters on a noviceship. An impediment to the noviceship is a circumstance affecting a person that would make his or her noviceship invalid (diriment impediment) or merely illicit (merely prohibiting impediment). All institutes of religious life are obliged by the diriment impediments of this canon. Some institutes have had additional impediments, both diriment and merely prohibiting, of their own proper law.

In the present matter a law produces only the common effect of a law when it is a merely prohibiting impediment: it prohibits but does not invalidate. To be a diriment impediment the law must state certainly and expressly that it is an invalidating law, e.g., by the phrases that a person is incapable of making a valid noviceship or cannot be validly admitted into the noviceship, that a personal circumstance was a diriment impediment or that no noviceship could exist because of the circumstance.

Invalidating laws are concerned only with juridical acts. These are acts that effect the acquisition, change and loss of rights and obligations, such as contracts, marriage, religious profession and the acquisition of an office, e.g., that of general superior. It is impossible to invalidate a simple act of disobedience, but marriage, since it produces the rights and obligations of husband and wife, can be invalidated.

Let us suppose that a religious profession is invalidly made. The invalidating law does not and cannot annihilate the physical entity of the act of profession, nor can it annul the moral entity of the act, that is, that the act was or was not knowingly and thus sinfully made contrary to law. However, the act of profession would otherwise have produced the rights and obligations of the religious state. The precise result of the invalidating law is to annul these effects. The one who made the invalid profession is not a religious and has none of the rights and obligations of a religious. Inculpable ignorance excuses from the sin but not from the invalidating effect of such laws. Ignorance would excuse also from the invalidity of a particular law if such a law stated that ignorance had this effect. None of the invalidating laws on the religious state admits ignorance as an excuse from the invalidating effect. The distinction between morality and invalidity can be seen more clearly, perhaps, when the law is invalidating but does not command or prohibit the particular act. An example of this is a civil law commanding that a will be in writing and not made merely orally. The sense of the law is that the testator is not obliged to make the will in writing but, if he does not do so, the will is destitute of effect and the property will be distributed according to the law of the state on those who die intestate.

Importance of Invalidating Laws. Members should faithfully observe all the laws of their institute and especially of the Church, but the invalidating laws are to be even more carefully studied and most strictly observed. Very serious consequences can arise from negligence in this matter, since the invalidating laws on the religious life can quite readily cause a chain of invalidity in the institute, e.g., an invalid noviceship makes all subsequent professions invalid (can. 656, 2°; 658, 2°). Such possible cases could be multiplied, and all possible cases appear to have been verified in fact. The care for the observance of invalidating laws in the religious life rarely falls on members or local superiors. It is the director of novices, higher superiors, their councilors and the general and provincial secretaries who must take care of the observance of such laws. They should know enough canon law to recognize or at least to suspect an invalidating law and they must seek competent advice in any doubtful matter.

643, § 1. *Canonical and Invalidating Impediments*. This canon establishes all its impediments as invalidating, unlike the 1917 code, which had both invalidating and merely prohibiting impediments. The following invalidly enter the noviceship:

1° *Age*. One who has not completed his 17th year, which is attained on the day after his 17th birthday, unless law established otherwise (see Chapter X).

2° *Marriage*, i.e., married persons as long as the bond of matrimony endures. Not an engagement nor the state of a widow or widower but any valid marriage still in existence, whether the other party consents or dissents to the entrance into any religious institute, is a diriment impediment to entrance into the noviceship. A marriage is presumed to be valid until it is declared invalid by the Church; it is still in existence until the death of either party or dissolution by the Church. Mere separation, even if the party who wishes to enter a religious institute is in no way culpable with regard to the separation, does not remove the impediment.

This impediment is now to be said to be indispensable. The SCRSI stated that it does not possess the faculty of dispensing. When a petition was forwarded to His Holiness, the Secretary of State replied, "after having considered everything well, it is not held as opportune to depart from the practice obtaining up to the present time [of not granting the dispensation]" (see CLD, 1980 Supplement, can. 542).

3° *Existing Membership in Another Institute*. The canon reads, "who is presently obligated by a sacred bond in an institute of consecrated life, or is incorporated into a society of apostolic life . . . " Therefore, the impediment is verified in those who are now, not merely in the past, bound by valid religious vows, solemn or simple, perpetual, definitive or temporary, or by any other bond of incorporation, perpetual, definitive or temporary, in a secular institute, whether either type of institute is pontifical or diocesan, clerical or lay, or a society of apostolic life. In the 1917 code the impediment extended also to those who had such a bond in the past. This restriction appears to diminish notably the practicality of the impediment.

"An institute" is apparently understood in 5° and inferentially also in 3° by the study group that composed the canons as "another institute." This is not completely clear in the original text ("aliquod institutum" and "aliquo instituto") and could and should have been made explicit, as suggested by one consultor and as found in can. 645, § 2 ("aliud institutum").

4° *Fraud and Coercion.* "who enters religion induced by force, grave fear, or fraud, or whom the superior receives under the pressure of the same influences." Physical violence and grave fear are of almost no practical importance in this matter and can be dispatched briefly. If one enters the noviceship or the competent higher superior admits to the noviceship when forced to do this act by physical violence or determined to it by the threat of a serious evil, the noviceship is invalid, no matter who is the cause of the physical violence or of the threat of serious evil.

Fraud is of practical importance. Fraud is any lie, concealment of truth, artifice, or subterfuge knowingly done to obtain admission or entrance to the noviceship with reference to things certainly requisite for admission or entrance, which would otherwise be denied. The effect of invalidity is the same, no matter who is the cause of the fraud, e.g., the superior admitting, the candidate himself or a third party. In actual practice the fraud will rarely be verified in anyone but the candidate.

Fraud demands in the perpetrator the certainty or at least the reasonable suspicion that the manifestation of the truth will preclude admission or entrance. All candidates should be prudently admonished at the time of the examination for admission of the possible effect of deceit and dissimulation. Fraud can be perpetrated against the higher superior to gain admission or against the candidate to secure his entrance. If the fraud causes a substantial error, the noviceship is invalid by the natural law. The error of a superior concerning the identity of the person being admitted and that of a candidate who believed she was entering an institute of common cloister, whereas it was actually one of papal cloister, have been given frequently as examples of substantial error.

The noviceship would have a twofold source of invalidity from canon law in the fraudulent concealment of a diriment impediment that is indispensable or when it is the will of the superior not to obtain a dispensation. The more usual object of fraud perpetrated against the superior admitting is had in physical, intellectual and moral requirements that are certainly requisite for admission in the mind of the superior. Fraud can readily be verified in the concealment of a physical infirmity that renders the candidate unfit for the life of the institute, that will readily incapacitate him, or that will cause great expense to the institute; in moral defects such as a habit of past drunkenness or of drug addiction, a conviction for a criminal offense, a marriage outside the Church, the bearing of a child outside of marriage, and in a notable family disgrace.

Fraud can also be exercised against a candidate, e.g., if parents falsely made their daughter believe that they had promised God that she would enter religion, or by falsely alleging poverty to induce their daughter to enter, or by anyone who falsely persuades another that he has evident signs of a religious vocation. In all cases the impediment of fraud does not exist unless the other requisite conditions given above are verified.

Fraud must be perpetrated against the superior who has the right of admitting to the noviceship. There will almost always be also a vote of the council or chapter, the latter in autonomous monasteries or houses. If the vote is consultative, the fraud must be exercised against the superior, since he alone admits in such a case. If the deliberative vote is prescribed, the superior in a way acts with his council or chapter, and the fraud must vitiate at least the number of votes that effect the majority. As long as any of the three influences mentioned retains its determining effect on the consent of the superior or novice, the noviceship is invalid. As soon as such an influence ceases and the superior or novice freely consents, the noviceship begins to run validly.

5° *Concealed Previous Incorporation.* The concealment must have been done knowingly. However, nothing in the wording of the canon implies a fraudulent concealment, i.e., the certainty or at least the suspicion that the manifestation of the truth would preclude admission. The sense also is of an actual incorporation into an institute of consecrated life (religious or secular institute) or a society of apostolic life. Again we have the same difficulty as under 3°—that the study group apparently understands the incorporation as that into another institute, even though this is not explicitly stated in the text.

§ 2. *Impediments of Proper Law*. As is evident, religious institutes may establish other invalidating entrance impediments. These should be established only if really necessary, and even then a merely prohibiting law would usually suffice. The canon also states that proper law may place invalidating conditions regarding entrance. Here also a mere prohibition would practically always suffice. Conditions may mean such things as a minimum level of education, a period of secular employment before entrance, and so forth.

Field of Proper Law. The field of proper law of a religious institute is: 1) matters over and above but not contrary to common law except when permitted by the latter or in virtue of a privilege; 2) proper laws may even be invalidating and, in a pontifical clerical institute, penal; 3) the members are obliged to obey proper law even though this obligation is not ordinarily immediately under sin in itself.

644. *Secular Clerics, Debtors*. Canon 644 states, "Superiors shall not admit secular clerics to the noviceship without consulting their ordinary nor those burdened with debts which they are unable to pay."

Converts. Converts, now Catholics, but unbaptized non-Catholics before conversion, and Catholics, formerly baptized but non-Catholics not in full communion with the Church before reception into it, should not be admitted until there is sufficient evidence of their constancy in faith and in religious vocation, but no determined period of time is required between reception into the Church and entrance into an institute. There is no mention of this matter in the canons.

645, § 1. *Certificates of Baptism, Confirmation, and Freedom of State*. The baptismal certificate will alone suffice if it also contains the notation of the reception of confirmation. If certificates cannot be obtained, the reception of either sacrament can be proved by the attestation of one perfectly trustworthy witness or by the candidate himself if he was baptized or confirmed after attaining the use of reason. If testimonials cannot be obtained immediately but it is certain that the candidate was baptized and confirmed, he may be admitted and the testimonials secured later. If he has not been confirmed and cannot conveniently receive confirmation before entrance, he may be admitted but he is to be confirmed as soon as possible. An attestation is also to be obtained of the freedom of a candidate from obstacles that would prevent his entrance.

§ 2. For the admission of clerics or those who had been admitted into another institute of consecrated life, into a society of apostolic life or a seminary, testimonials are further required respectively of the local ordinary, major superior of the institute or society, or rector of the seminary.

§ 3. *Other Testimonials*. The proper law, as also the admitting higher superior may demand other testimonials concerning the required suitability and the freedom of candidates from impediments, e.g., the consent of parents or guardians and diplomas or certificates of studies and academic degrees.

§ 4. Finally, the canon affirms, "Superiors may also seek other information, even under secrecy, if they believe this necessary."

Formation of Novices

646. This canon on the purpose of the noviceship is most important but its sense is evident from a mere reading.

647, § 1. *Establishment, Transfer and Disestablishment of a Novitiate*. The terms, "erection" and "suppression," apply properly to an institute, province or house, not to a novitiate. I am therefore avoiding them in a matter that can readily be confused. A novitiate is obviously in a house; even the entire house may be a novitiate. However, the house and the novitiate are always two distinct things. The present canon is not treating of a house as such, which has already been done in can. 609 and

616. The designation of a novitiate does not create a new juridical person as does the erection of a house, but merely authoritatively designates a house or part of a house as officially suitable for the specific purpose of the formation of novices. It is understood that an autonomous monastery or house of its nature as the one house possesses the right to have its own novitiate without any formal designation. One may doubt that the formality of writing in the prescript of a "written decree" is required for validity. The canon enacts that the competent authority for the establishment, transfer or disestablishment of any novitiate in the institute is the general superior with the consent of his council and by a written decree. The constitutions will usually require the previous petition by the provincial superior with the deliberative or consultative vote of his council for the same acts.

§§ 2-3. *Noviceship and Periods Outside the Novitiate.* For its validity, i.e., the twelve months prescribed by can. 648, § 1, the noviceship must be made in a house legitimately designated for this purpose. Exceptionally a novice may be permitted to make his noviceship in another house of the institute. The novitiate group, the director, his assistants and the novices, may be permitted to reside during some periods in another house of the institute. In both cases the requisites, which are clearly stated in the canon, must be observed. Neither material nor social separation of the novice from the professed nor the dress of novices is imposed by canon law but norms of proper law on these matters may be enacted.

648, § 1. *Duration of the Noviceship.* The duration must be twelve months, but it is not commanded that these be continuous; they may be broken by periods of apostolic activity. If this time is continuous, the computation is the same as in the past, according to can. 203, § 2. Therefore, the prescribed duration, if begun on August 14, 1985, ends on August 15, 1986, or more exactly at midnight of August 14-15, 1986. If broken, e.g., by apostolic periods, the 12 months are computed according to can. 202, § 1. A month is then a space of 30 days, and 12 months are 360 days. The requisite of the canon, "in the novitiate community itself," includes the novitiate house. The same principle is applied to the two cases of a permissible noviceship or period of noviceship outside the novitiate house of the preceding can. 647, §§ 2-3. (see Chapter X on computing time).

A longer period of noviceship, such as 6 months or the far more common second year, is computed as in the past according to the proper law or usage. The norms of canon law do not touch it, and in fact norms are not found on this matter in proper law, at least of lay institutes. Proper law has in the past and should require such additional time only for the liceity of the noviceship.

§ 2. *Periods of Apostolic Activity.* As understood in the past, the purpose of such periods outside the novitiate house was not primarily technical nor professional training but to help the novice "to better discover the exigencies of their vocation as religious and how to remain faithful to them" (*Renovationis causam*, no. 5). No restrictions are placed by the canon on these periods, except that the time spent in them must be added to the prescribed 12 months, nor may they be contrary to can . 648, § 3, which limits the noviceship to a maximum of two years. They may be one or many periods, during or after the prescribed twelve months. The preceding law required that they be begun only after a novice had spent three months in the novitiate, postulated a minimum of six continuous months in the novitiate, and a return there of at least a month before the first profession. Such periods may be used for one, several or the entire group of novices. The periods are obviously to be used so that they help, not obstruct, the spiritual formation of the novices. Such periods do not apply to contemplative institutes.

§ 3. *Noviceship Not To Be Longer Than Two Years.* The noviceship, inclusive of the periods of apostolic activity, must not be longer than two years. However, it may be beyond this maximum of two years in a prolongation of the noviceship. Can. 653, § 2 declares, "If his suitability is doubtful, the time of the noviceship may be prolonged according to the norm of proper law, but not beyond six months." This prolongation may be made even if the prescribed duration of the noviceship is two years. Prolongation, therefore, is not excluded nor lessened by the two-year maximum duration of the noviceship established in the present can. 648. This was also the norm of the former code.

649, § 1. *Absence During the Noviceship.* An absence from the novitiate house that exceeds 3 continuous or interrupted months from the 12 prescribed by can. 648, § 1 renders the noviceship invalid, which must consequently be begun again. A lesser absence but over 15 days is to be supplied, i.e., added to the noviceship. This supplying is not required for the validity of the noviceship because the canon does not here contain an invalidating clause, as in can. 556, § 2 of the 1917 code.

Exceeds 3 Months. The absence is one that exceeds 90 days, if the time of the absence is not continuous; but if it is a continuous absence, the norm of can. 203, § 2 would be applied, i.e., an absence begun on March 28 would attain 3 full months at midnight of June 28-9, i.e., 92 days, unless otherwise established in law (see Chapter X). Any absence must be from the novitiate house, not merely from the novitiate part of the house. This same principle is to apply to the two legitimate houses for a noviceship described in can. 647, §§ 2-3. The reason for the absence is immaterial.

§ 2. *Anticipation of First Profession.* With the permission of the major superior competent by determination of proper law, first profession may be anticipated but not beyond 15 days. This is an actual abbreviation of the noviceship, whether this is of 12 months or longer. Therefore, a first profession to be made on August 15 could be anticipated back to July 31. The required permission of the competent major superior implies the necessity of a sufficient reason for the anticipation.

650, §§ 1-2. *Formation and Government Appertain to the Director of Novices.* The same Latin term is used as in the past, *magister*. It may consequently be translated as master or mistress, director or directress. Both the government and the formation of the novices appertain exclusively to the director under the authority of higher superiors. Assistant directors are made subject to the director in both fields by can. 651, § 2. The proper law of an institute, unless founded on a privilege, may give no authority in this matter to the minor local superior. Matters that affect the house as such, e.g., the time of Mass, meals and similar matters, appertain to the government and decisions of the minor local superior. Mutual consultation should preclude any difficulties in such matters. The canon makes it clear that it is the director of novices, not a formation team, that directs the novitiate. The latter may certainly be consulted.

650, § 1. *Formation Program.* This is stated to be "according to the program of formation defined by proper law." It is understood that the formation will be primarily according to canon law, e.g., can. 646 on the purpose of the noviceship, and 652, § 2 on broad principles of formation. Secondly, the formation must be according to any instructions issued by Roman Congregations, and even more by the teaching of the Roman Pontiffs on religious life and formation. The broad principles of formation should be in the constitutions, the lesser principles and details in the directory.

651, § 1. *Qualities and Designation of the Director.* The first paragraph of this canon demands that the director be a member of the institute and have made perpetual profession. Other qualities are to be prescribed by proper law, e.g., a determined number of years of perpetual profession. Obviously proper law should prescribe the qualities required by the nature of this important office. The canon then enjoins that the director be legitimately designated. He may therefore be appointed or elected. Election has been the established method in some autonomous monasteries but most rarely in centralized institutes. I do not believe a chapter to be a good judge of specialized abilities. The common form of designation of the director has been by the appointment of a higher superior.

In the past, at least with regard to lay institutes of simple vows, the practice was that the director and his assistant, when there were no provinces, were appointed by the general superior with the consent of his council. The same norm prevailed in institutes divided into provinces, especially with regard to the director. These institutes frequently enacted that the names were to be proposed by the provincial council or by the provincial alone or that either of these was to be consulted before the appointment. Infrequently they were appointed by the provincial with the consent of his council, but this act had to be confirmed by the general superior with the consent of his council or the general superior alone. A few institutes required no such confirmation. In a small number of institutes, the appointment was by the provincial superior alone. In autonomous monasteries, these two officials were more frequently appointed by the local major superior with the consent of the council, in some with the advice of the council, by election in or with the consent or advice of the chapter.

§ 3. *Preparation of Novitiate Staff.* The director and his assistants should be selected for their competence, be properly prepared, free of any other assignment that could impede their work, be dedicated to the work, and not changed with unwise frequency.

652, § 1. *Discernment of Vocations.* The more proximate discernment of vocations appertains to the director and his assistants, but the official discernment to the higher superior who admits to first profession assisted by his council.

Noviceship for One Class Is Valid for Another Class. The usual classes are clerical members and lay brothers, if these are distinct classes in a particular institute; choir and lay nuns and extern sisters. It is also possible that teaching and nursing sisters and lay sisters may be found. A proposed canon had stated that, unless the constitutions enacted the contrary, a noviceship made for one class was valid for another. This canon was later suppressed by the Roman study group, but all its statements remain true because they are neither invalidated nor otherwise excluded by any other canon. The same is true of the time period in temporary vows in one class because the canons do not exclude this.

If the passing is done during the noviceship, the full time of the noviceship is to be completed; if during the time of temporary vows, the full time of temporary vows is to be completed. The higher superior competent to permit the transfer is the one who, with any prescribed vote, has the right of admitting to the noviceship, temporary profession, or perpetual profession of the new class, according to whether the transfer is made during the noviceship, temporary vows or after definitive or perpetual vows. No new profession appears to be necessary because of the transfer. All that is necessary is the consent of the member and the permission of the competent higher superior.

653, § 1. *Right of Novice to Leave.*

1) *Voluntary Departure.* The freedom of a novice to leave at any time and of one in temporary vows to do so at the end of any temporary profession has been explained above under can. 642. Dismissal of a novice, of its nature as an expulsion from the whole institute and province and not merely from a house, appertains to higher superiors.

2) *Dismissal.* Dismissal should have been effected as soon as a novice was found certainly unsuitable. Superiors are at least ordinarily to urge a novice to leave voluntarily before resorting to dismissal. It is understood that there exists at least a just reason for dismissal. This will be, at least ultimately, the lack of a vocation to the religious life or that of the particular institute. A dismissal for an insufficient reason is valid. According to the practice of the SCRSI, the dismissal of a novice is reserved to higher superiors with the vote of the council, which is more frequently consultative than deliberative.

In institutes without provinces, the competent higher superior is necessarily the general superior. In institutes with provinces, the right is more frequently reserved to the general superior, but in some institutes it is assigned to the higher or provincial superior. When the right is reserved to the general superior, the constitutions at times prescribe that the provincial and his council are to be consulted, which in practice should always be done. In autonomous houses and monasteries, the right of dismissal is given to the local major superior, usually with the consent of the council or chapter.

§ 2. *End of the Noviceship.* If found certainly suitable, a novice is to be admitted to first profession and thus to membership in the institute. If found unsuitable, he is to be excluded from first profession. If doubtfully suitable, the competent higher superior may, but is not obliged to, prolong the noviceship, which he may not do for more than six months. A novice who has been excluded without such a prolongation is thus expelled from the institute. It is also evident that exclusion is merely the correlative or synonym for non-admission to profession and, of its nature, appertains to the act of admission. The higher superior who admits to first profession is the one who excludes from first profession.

Prolongation or Extension of the Noviceship. A prolongation of the noviceship or of temporary vows is to be avoided as far as possible. Unsatisfactory novices and professed of temporary vows should be promptly instructed, counseled, and admonished. Prolongation of either state is rarely found to be a satisfactory experiment except in some cases of health. Can. 653, § 2 does not permit a prolongation of the noviceship beyond six months, but the same length of prolongation is permitted also when the institute has a noviceship of two years. Constitutions are found, though rarely, that restrict the right of prolongation, e.g., to three months.

The prolongation need not necessarily be made for the full six months but may be made for a lesser period. A novice, if found satisfactory, may be admitted to first profession before the expiration of the time for which the prolongation had been made. The canon states that the reason for a prolongation is a doubt about the suitability of a novice for first profession. The sufficient reason for a prolongation must therefore be at least reducible to a doubt about the suitability of a novice. The request of the novice for further time for deliberation is such a reason.

Competent Superior for Prolongation. As stated above, the competent higher superior for exclusion of a novice should be the same as the one competent for admission to first profession. Admission and exclusion of their nature appertain to the same process because exclusion is merely the refusal of admission. If a novice is not admitted to first profession, he is excluded from the noviceship. We believe the same higher superior should be the one competent for the prolongation of the noviceship, since this is so closely connected with admission and exclusion and to the official discussion on these.

Because the 1917 code treated exclusion in such a distinct manner from admission, the practice has varied with regard to the necessity of a vote of the council of the competent higher superior from no vote to a consultative or deliberative vote for prolongation of the noviceship. This wide choice is permitted by can. 653, § 2, which leaves the entire matter of the superior competent for prolongation and the necessity of a vote of a council or chapter to the constitutions. We think that the vote should be deliberative. This will tend to eliminate prolongations that are too facile, imprudent, and sentimental rather than realistic. It would likewise make more difficult the ignoring of the vote of a council in a very important matter.

CHAPTER V

RELIGIOUS PROFESSION

654. *Profession, Consecration, Incorporation.* Religious profession demands the evangelical counsels of chastity, poverty and obedience, to which are added, also as public vows, any special vows in existence in a particular institute. Consecration, or a setting apart to God and divine things, is verified by the evangelical counsels, whose primary purpose is to control the principal obstacles to the perfection of the love of God, the infused virtue of charity. God invites to and accepts this consecration and he is thus the one who consecrates. Explicit or implicit incorporation accompanies a religious profession and consists of becoming a member of a religious institute and consequently of the acquisition of the rights and obligations of a member.

Every religious profession must be by public vows, which were and are defined: *"A vow is public if it is received in the name of the Church by a legitimate superior; otherwise it is private."* The vows, the consecrating element, are thus received by a higher superior of the institute but in the name of the Church, in virtue also of power received from the Church, and therefore through its ministry. The individual is consecrated to and directly obliged to God by the vows. By religious profession he at least implicitly enters and is accepted as a member of the particular religious institute and constituted in the religious state, with all the rights and obligations determined by canon and proper law. All religious professions, temporary or perpetual, must be by public vows. No other form of sacred bond is permitted. Solemn vows are not even mentioned in the present canon law on religious.

655. *Temporary Profession.* The novice is to make first temporary profession after the prescribed noviceship and for the time defined in proper law. Three years of temporary vows are required for the validity of perpetual profession (see can. 658, 2°) and the total time enacted in proper law for temporary vows may not be longer than six years. Six years therefore are the normal limit. Only in a prolongation, according to can. 657, § 2, may temporary vows be extended to nine years.

We believe that the prescribed duration of temporary vows should be five years, a prolongation should be no longer than a year, and that the first temporary profession should be for 2, the second for 3 years. If circumstances of the particular institute demand it, we would agree to a first profession for 3, a second for 2 years.

Canon law demands 3 years of temporary vows. Proper law, but prudently only for the liceity of perpetual profession, may require a period of 4, 5, or 6 years. Proper law may enact that there be only one profession, e.g., of 3 years, or even only one of 6 years. We would not consider the latter prudent. Proper law may also establish various durations of professions, e.g., six annual professions, three of 2 years each, two of 3 years, one of 2 years and the other of 4, etc. We do not believe that a temporary profession may be for an indefinite period on the part of the one taking the vows, such as, "for as long as I remain in this institute but not beyond six years."

The canons omit the former can. 577, § 2, "For a just reason superiors may permit the renewal of temporary vows to be anticipated but not by more than a month." However, the faculty remains because it does not abbreviate the time of temporary profession, provided the intention of the one renewing is that the anticipated renewal begins to run from the time a non-anticipated renewal would have begun to run. The requisite intention in any temporary profession or renewal in the one making profession and the superior admitting and receiving has been explained above under can. 607.

The formula of profession should be included in the constitutions. The other distinctive details of the rite may be placed in the directory or a ceremonial. The common rite of profession is found in the booklet, *Rite of Profession* (Washington, D. C., United States Catholic Conference, 1971). In this work, the opening decree of the Sacred Congregation for Divine Worship makes it clear that the rite of profession of each institute should be approved by the Sacred Congregation for Religious and Secular Institutes.

The latter congregation has stated more than once that the formula of profession may not be left to the free initiative of each individual but must be substantially the same for the entire institute, because of the identity of rights and duties deriving from profession. The individuals may add some expressions of their own will or devotion at the beginning or end of the approved formula. The addition should be distinguished by moderation and clarity and be completely consonant with the gravity and solemnity of the act they are preparing themselves to accomplish.

Obligations and Rights of the Professed. By his profession the novice becomes a member of the ecclesial religious state and is henceforth a subject of the rights and obligations of canon and common law affecting his state and to the legitimate authorities of that state, the Roman Pontiff as his highest internal superior, the SCRSI and other relevant Roman Congregations, diocesan bishops and other local ordinaries within their competence over the religious life. He likewise becomes the subject of the rights and obligations contained in the proper law of his institute, as he is also subject to the superiors and chapters of this institute.

Obligations of an Institute Consequent Upon Membership. The primary obligation is that of forming, directing and governing the member according to the life, laws and spirit of the religious state and of the particular institute. The new member hands over all his activity to the institute and acquires all property for his institute except personal gifts. Therefore, if he leaves or is dismissed, he cannot seek compensation for his work in the institute. The institute has the consequent obligation of providing his sustenance and material needs but according to the limits determined by proper law.

656. *Diriment Impediments to Any Temporary Profession.* This canon lists the diriment, or invalidating, impediments and conditions of canon law, which are in addition to the conditions demanded by the proper

constitutions. The latter may be added for validity or only liceity, and we recommend that they be enacted only for liceity if at all. The impediments of the canon are:

1° *Completion of at Least the Eighteenth Year*

2° *The Noviceship Validly Made According to the Norm of Law.* This means the completion of the canonical 12 months of noviceship demanded for its validity by can. 648, § 1, as also the fulfillment of any other laws or conditions required for the validity of the noviceship by canon law or the proper law of an institute.

3° *Admission Freely Made by the Competent Superior with the Vote of His Council According to the Norm of Law.* Admission to profession is the juridical act, previous to the actual profession, by which the competent higher superior decides that an individual (a novice or professed of temporary vows) may make a particular profession.

Competent Higher Superior. Can. 641 states that it appertains to major, or higher, superiors to admit to the noviceship. Therefore, admission to the first temporary profession, renewals of the preceding, and perpetual profession a fortiori appertains to higher superiors, as do prolongations of the noviceship or temporary profession, and reception of any profession. From their nature also, these acts transcend the limits of purely local government because they concern admission into an institute, not merely a house, and possibly also into a province. All further determinations of the competent higher superior and of the vote of the council as consultative or deliberative appertain to the proper constitutions.

The competent higher superior is necessarily the local higher superior in an autonomous house or monastery and the general superior in a centralized institute without provinces. In institutes with provinces, constitutions of the past frequently reserved admission to all professions to the general superior. Frequently also the right of admission was given to the provincial superior or higher superiors. Often also, especially for perpetual profession, the provincial admitted but his admission had to be confirmed by the general superior. In a few institutes, at least some admissions appertained to the general superior, but the request for admission was made by the provincial superior. Prolongation of the noviceship should appertain to the higher superior who admits to first profession, and of temporary profession to the higher superior who admits to perpetual profession.

Vote of the Council or Chapter. Canon law had demanded a deliberative vote of the council or chapter for admission to first profession, permitted either vote for perpetual profession, and did not require a vote for renewal or prolongation of temporary profession (can. 575, § 2). In the practice of the Roman Congregations in approving constitutions, the vote of the council or chapter was necessarily deliberative for first profession, commonly consultative for renewal. For prolongation the constitutions frequently demanded no vote but some required the consultative and a few the deliberative vote; finally, for perpetual profession the vote was practically always consultative.

In our judgment the vote of the council or chapter should be deliberative for first and perpetual professions, prolongation of profession (see can. 657, § 2), and consultative for renewals of profession. The final profession should clearly be by deliberative rather than the common consultative vote of the past. There is a modern tendency, not unknown in the past, to consult also some or all members of the community in which he is living or has lived on the suitability of an individual for profession.

The act of admission must have been free of physical violence, grave fear or fraud (see can. 643, § 1, 4° above).

4° *Profession Made Expressly and Freely.* The profession must be made explicitly or implicitly; a tacit profession is invalid. The profession is ordinarily made explicitly, i.e., "I vow chastity, poverty and obedience." It may be implicit, e.g., "I promise obedience according to the Rule of St. Augustine and the constitutions of the Order of Preachers." The other two vows are contained in and manifested by the words, "Rule" and "constitutions." Canon law had and excludes here a tacit profession, evidently because of the difficulty in proving that it was made. A tacit profession would consist externally in placing acts proper to the professed. If an individual, after completing the noviceship, put on the habit of the professed, it would have been presumed that he intended to assume the rights and obligations of the professed. The one making the profession must be free in making it from physical violence, grave fear or fraud (see 643, § 1, 4° above).

5° *The Profession Must Have Been Received by the Legitimate Superior Personally or Through Another.* It seems to us again that reception of public vows in a religious institute is a matter that transcends purely local government and pertains of its nature to the higher superior determined by the constitutions. This is also the practice of the Roman Congregations in approving constitutions. According to this practice, when there are no provinces, the vows are received by the general superior or his delegate. This is also true very frequently in institutes divided into provinces, but in these the legitimate higher superior is often expressed as a higher superior or a provincial. Different superiors are at times assigned for various professions, e.g., the general superior for perpetual profession and the provincials for the profession of and renewals of temporary professions. It is the clear sense of the law that reception of vows appertains to internal government and that it can be possessed by an extern, even a bishop, only by delegation from a competent member of the institute. The one delegated should ordinarily, although not necessarily always, be a member of the same institute.

Delegation. The higher superior designated in the constitutions for the reception of vows may delegate this faculty in whole or in part. For example, if the general superior is so designated, he may delegate the provincials to receive all vows in their provinces and local superiors all vows in their houses. One who has ordinary power, as the general superior above, or habitual delegation, as the provincials and local superiors above, may delegate or sub-delegate others to receive the vows in particular cases. A delegation to receive all the professions at a determined ceremony is a delegation in a particular case. If a local superior has been habitually delegated to receive the vows in his house, he may sub-delegate another to receive all the vows at a determined ceremony, e.g., that of August 15, 1985. However, one who is sub-delegated to receive the vows cannot again sub-delegate his power unless he has expressly received the faculty to do so from one with ordinary power (can. 137, § 4).

It is especially to be noted that renewals of temporary vows are to be received. In the past there was at times a failure to do this because the juridical renewal was identified with a merely devotional renewal. The following typical article in the constitutions would assure the presence always of one competent for reception: "(Provincials, regional and local) superiors and their legitimate substitutes are delegated by the constitutions to receive all professions in their (provinces, regions and) houses, and with power also to subdelegate." A priest celebrates the Mass and presides over the ceremonies. He does not as such receive the vows. The reception of the vows does not have to be expressed orally but is sufficiently manifested by the presence of the designated higher superior or legitimate delegate. Any verbal form of reception required by the rite of the institute is obviously to be observed.

657, § 1. *Admission to or Exclusion From a Further Profession.* At the completion of a period of temporary profession, a member judged suitable, who voluntarily requests it, is to be admitted by the higher superior competent according to proper law to a renewal of temporary vows or perpetual profession. If he is not so admitted and there is no prolongation of temporary vows, he is excluded from and is to leave the institute. In brief, if renewal alone is denied or if perpetual admission is denied without prolongation, the member by that very fact is excluded from and is to leave the institute.

§ 2. *Prolongation of Temporary Vows.* This may not be done for a period that would result in a total time in temporary vows beyond nine years. A prescribed profession of temporary vows for five years, may be prolonged for but not beyond four years. Ordinarily a prolongation has been done for a year at a time. "If it seems appropriate," is the reason that the canon requires for a prolongation. Prolongation should not be employed unless there are founded reasons for judging that the member will overcome the obstacles to perpetual profession through the prolongation. Prolongation can be justifiable. It can also be harmful to the individual and the institute by the retention of an unsuitable member in a state of probation. It is necessary to emphasize that God does not call, elect, or choose for a life of counsel those who are unsuited for it.

§ 3. *Anticipation of Perpetual Profession.* This may be done for a just reason but not beyond three months, even if the institute requires only three years of temporary vows. The major superior competent for anticipation must be determined by proper law (see can. 649, § 2).

658. *Requisites for the Validity of Perpetual Profession.* The following are required in addition to those enumerated in can. 656, §§ 3, 4, and 5, and those established in proper law.

1) *At least the completed twenty-first year of age.*

2) *A previous temporary profession of at least three years, the permissible anticipation of three months of can. 657, § 3 being maintained.*

It is to be noted that an invalid noviceship invalidates the entire time spent presumably in temporary vows (see can. 656, 2°) and consequently also the perpetual profession by the lack of at least three full years of temporary profession.

Formation of Professed Members

659-61. These canons describe in general terms the initial and ongoing spiritual, apostolic and professional formation of professed members of the religious life. The detailed description of this matter appertains more to an instruction of the relevant Roman Congregations than to universal law, which will be published after the promulgation of the new canon law. The broad principles of formation should be in the constitutions, the details, as sufficiently changeable matter, in the directory.

According to these canons, the spiritual formation is to be completed after the noviceship to enable the members to live adequately the life and purpose of the institute. Proper law is to define the duration and program of the formation, adapted to the needs of the Church, the conditions of persons and of times. Those in the formation program are not to be given assignments that would impede their formation. This formation should be theoretical and practical, according to the demands of the institute.

Appropriate degrees are to be obtained. The formation of those destined for Holy Orders is regulated by the program of studies of the universal law and of the institute. Throughout their lives, the members should earnestly further their spiritual, doctrinal, and professional development, and superiors should provide them with the means and time for this end as far as they can.

266. § 1. *Affiliation to an Institute as a Cleric.* By the reception of the diaconate, one becomes a cleric and is incardinated in the particular church or personal prelature for whose service he was promoted.

§ 2. A member of a religious institute, professed of perpetual vows or definitively incorporated in a clerical society of apostolic life, by the reception of the diaconate is incardinated as a cleric in the same institute or society, unless the constitutions are to the contrary in the society.

§ 3. By the reception of the diaconate a member of a secular institute is incardinated in the particular church for whose service he was promoted, unless he is incardinated in the institute itself in virtue of a concession of the Apostolic See.

CHAPTER VI

THE RIGHTS AND OBLIGATIONS
OF RELIGIOUS INSTITUTES
AND THEIR MEMBERS

662. *Christ the Supreme Rule of Religious*. This spiritual canon has also a juridical aspect in the repetition of the Vatican II statement on the place of the Rule and constitutions in the religious life, *"The members should regard as the supreme rule of their lives the following of Christ as set forth in the gospel"* (PC, no. 2). We have often been inclined to hold that this is the most valuable sentence in Vatican II for the religious life. It brings out the previously almost unspoken fact that the Rule and constitutions are not ends in themselves nor closed in on themselves but means to the loving and living of the person Christ. To be a Benedictine, Franciscan or Jesuit is not the great thing but to be a better Christian through being a Benedictine, Franciscan or Jesuit.

The past manner of looking on the Rule and constitutions opened the way to legalism in the religious life. It was the observance of law, rule and regulation that was often made primary, which tended to dry up the living of the person Christ. The religious was called a regular because he observed a Rule (*regula*). The members should more clearly show forth Christ to the world day by day. In other words they should daily and more progressively witness more completely to Christ. This is the duty of the disciple of Christ, "Everywhere on earth they must bear witness to Christ . . ." (LG, no. 10).

We witness to Christ by living Christ, by making every action that which Christ himself would place in the same circumstances. This

comes about through grace; the illumination and inspiration of the Holy
Spirit, who teaches us Christ, as the Paraclete who will "remind you of
all that I told you" (Jn 14:26); through prayer and constant effort and
union. By these we grow into Christ's way of thinking, loving and
desiring and consequently into his way of acting. It is a good thing to
study the whole spiritual life in the abstract, e.g., the goal of perfect
charity and the fact that the evangelical counsels are means to the end;
but we live these to live Christ, we are chaste to live Christ and to do it
more completely. It seems to us that a synthesis of the charism, spirit and
individuality should appear prominently in the constitutions, and its
connection with living Christ should be stated even more prominently.

663-64. *Spiritual Principles and Exercises.* Most of what is given in
these canons is self-evident. It is obvious that participation in the Mass
should be the principal part of the day of all religious. Vatican II stated of
priests: "Priests fulfill their chief duty in the mystery of the Eucharistic
Sacrifice. In it the work of our redemption continues to be carried out.
For this reason, priests are strongly urged to celebrate Mass every day,
for even if the faithful are unable to be present, it is an act of Christ and of
the Church" (PO, no. 13). In the document on *Liturgical Formation in
Seminaries*, we read: " . . . the Church emphatically recommends a daily
celebration of the Eucharistic Sacrifice by priests, even if they are not
held to this by a pastoral obligation or if the presence of the faithful
cannot be had, as the act of Christ and the Church and offered for the
salvation of the entire world" (*Notitiae*, 15 [1979], 535). One also
adores the Lord in the Sacrament during visits, benediction and other
exercises. The relator of the study group gave the reply that "frequently" regarding confession has the same meaning as now, i.e., every
two weeks.

Obligation of Praying the Liturgy of the Hours. The United States
Bishops' Committee on the Liturgy stated the obligation of clerics as
follows:

1. The General Instruction on the Liturgy of the Hours, replacing the
canons of 1917, defined the obligation of priests and deacons as that "of
reciting the canonical hours in their entirety each day according to one's

proper and approved liturgical books," and to do this while respecting as far as possible the relation of the several hours of prayer to the appropriate times of the day.

2. The United States Conference of Bishops has merely *encouraged* permanent deacons to pray the morning and evening prayer. It is stated to be appropriate that this be done with their families.

3. The varying weight of the different liturgical hours and priorities among them are to be judged reasonably and without scruples.

4. Neither morning nor evening prayer should be omitted except for serious reasons and thus only exceptionally. The judgment of such seriousness is left to the cleric.

5. A lesser than the serious reasons of the preceding norm justifies the omission of the office of readings.

6. The clerics "will also have at heart the recitation" of the daytime prayer and of night prayer, or compline. Therefore, these are not stated to be obligatory.

7. Effective November 27, 1977, only the Liturgy of the Hours, as it appears in several authorized editions of the *Liturgia Horarum* may be used for liturgical observance, whether in common or by individuals, of the Church's office of prayer according to the Roman Rite (see RfR, 38 [1979], 69-70; *General Instruction on the Liturgy of the Hours*, nos. 29-30; can. 276, § 2, 3°).

Liturgy of the Hours in the Religious Life. The following are the pertinent norms of the *General Instruction on the Liturgy of the Hours.* "Communities of canons, monks, nuns, and other religious who by virtue of their Rule or constitutions celebrate the Liturgy of the Hours either in whole or in part according to the common or a special rite represent the praying Church in a special way . . . This may be said especially of those who are engaged in the contemplative life" (no. 24). "Religious communities bound to recite the Liturgy of the Hours and their individual members are to celebrate the hours in accord with the norms of their particular law . . . " (no. 31, b). "Communities bound to choir recitation are to recite the whole course of the hours daily in choir. Outside of choir, however, individual members recite the hours according to the norms of their particular law . . ." (no. 31, b).

665, § 1. *Faculty to Permit Absences.* Religious are enjoined in this paragraph to reside, as flowing from common life, in their own house and not to depart from it without the permission of their superior. The canon is not talking of brief absences, and the norms for these appertain to proper law. The canon authorizes a major superior, with the consent of his or her council, to permit a member to reside outside a house of his or her institute for as long as the case requires when the reason is the cure of an infirmity, studies, or an apostolate to be exercised in the name of the institute. The secretary and a consultor of the Roman study group stated that the apostolate intended was not any personal apostolate at all freely chosen by the religious himself. The infirmity or illness here is one afflicting the religious, not a member of his family or other relatives. The requirement of the consent of the council manifests the careful thought that should be given to many of the cases of such apostolates.

Any other prolonged absence must be for a just reason, not for more than a year, and likewise be given by a major superior with the consent of his council. The concession obviously does not have to be and often should not be for a full year. The more common reasons now proposed are a vocational decision and the care of a seriously ill or infirm father or mother. The latter is much more apt to occur when the religious is a woman. One often wonders why the other family members cannot collectively employ a secular person for such care. Such a plan has to be followed when none of the family members is a sister.

A religious has given herself to a perpetually consecrated life, and she should not be considered by her family or herself as always available for such care. A vocational decision can almost always be settled in one's own religious house. Untold thousands of men and women decide to marry while living the usual family life. Very long absences have been the result in many of these two types of cases. They too demand serious thought and the consent of the council. The higher superior is granted no authority to renew this permission. The permission should be granted by a major superior with the supernatural good of the religious very prominently in mind. The absence is not to be regarded as something of a sabbatical year from community life to which all religious have a right. When granted loosely, these absences quickly multiply, and the roster of the institute has a formidable list of furloughed or "leave of absence" members.

Obviously a member remains such during his absence and is held to the observance of his vows, as also other obligations except those incompatible with the state of absence, such as the community exercises. Unless the superior has established other financial arrangements, the authorized indult of absence implicitly gives him permission to acquire, administer, and use temporal goods insofar as these are necessary for his becoming maintenance and for the purpose of the indult, e.g., the support of parents. He remains under the authority of superiors and retains active and passive voice during the absence.

The retention of active and passive voice can cause difficulties. One author permits the major superior to demand that the member resign any office he holds and renounce active and passive voice in any relevant case as a condition of granting the permission for the absence (Escudero, *Il nuovo diritto dei religiosi*, Rome: *Commentarium pro Religiosis*, 1973, no. 222). This opinion may be followed. In revising constitutions, religious institutes may add, e.g., the prescript that religious who have been granted permission of a prolonged absence and those who have petitioned an indult of secularization (departure) are deprived of any office they hold and also of active and passive voice. The latter right will be regained on their return from the absence.

§ 2. *Members Illegitimately Absent.* These members may be of perpetual or temporary vows. Without permission they leave their religious institute or, having licitly left, they remain outside of it without permission with the intention of withdrawing themselves from the authority of superiors.

1. *Obligations of the Offenders.* The offenders described above are freed from none of the obligations of their institute and are consequently obliged by its vows and proper law. They have a serious obligation in conscience to return as soon as it is morally possible to their institute. To be worthy of sacramental absolution, they must actually return, sincerely

intend to return or at least sincerely intend to submit themselves to the direction of their superiors. If the offender states that he can no longer fulfill the obligations of the religious life, the formalities for an indult of departure are to be initiated. If the return of such an offender involves a grave inconvenience, superiors may permit him to remain outside the institute until the indult of departure has been obtained.

2. *Obligations of Superiors.* All superiors of such an offender but primarily the immediate higher superior are obliged to find him, effect his return and receive him back if he is sincerely repentant. Superiors may fulfill their obligation personally or through another. At times another member, a priest, friend or relative may have greater influence with the offender. The seeking of the offender is always to be done with prudence and charity, i.e., with the avoidance of scandal, infamy or hardship to either the offender or the institute. The obligation of seeking these offenders binds only when and as long as there is probable hope that they will amend and return.

3. *Repentant Offenders.* The institute is obliged to take back an offender only if he is sincerely repentant. The institute has the right of proving the sincerity of his repentance by a period of trial. If sincere repentance is lacking, the superior should counsel the member to ask for an indult of departure or, if he will not do this, begin the formalities of dismissal. If he appears repentant but his return and presence can be a cause of trouble to the institute and superiors find serious difficulty in receiving him back, they may defer the return, present the facts to the SCRSI, and await its decision.

4. *Offender Unwilling to Return.* If the offender is unwilling to return, superiors should counsel him to request an indult of departure; if he will not do this, they are to resort to dismissal.

666. *Necessary Discretion Regarding Means of Communication.* The words and principals of Paul VI, in an allocution of May 23, 1964, are applicable here.

"Everybody knows that in the prevailing conditions of human society the practice of perfect chastity is made difficult, not only because of the prevalence of low morals but also on account of false teachings which glamorize excessively the merely natural and pour deadly poison into the souls of men. This state of affairs should rouse religious to greater and greater faith—that faith by which we believe the words of Christ when he proclaims the supernatural value of chastity that is sought for the sake of the kingdom of heaven, that state which assures us beyond doubt that, with the help of divine grace, we can preserve unsullied the flower of chastity.

"To attain this happy ideal it is necessary to practice Christian mortification with greater zeal and also to exercise custody of the senses with more diligent care. Therefore, the life of the religious should find no place for books, periodicals, or shows which are unbecoming or indecent, not even under the pretext of a desire to learn things useful to know or to broaden one's cultural outlook. Excepted possibly is the case, examined and approved by the religious superior, where there is proven necessity for the study of such things. In a world steeped in so many forms of vice, no one can really evaluate the effectiveness of the sacred ministry of one whose life is radiant with the light of chastity consecrated to God and from which he draws his strength" (Bouscaren-O'Connor, *Canon Law Digest*, 6, 429).

667, §§ 1-2. *Necessity of Cloister.* Cloister must be observed in all houses according to the determination of proper law and in keeping with the character and mission of the institute. The present common cloister would appear to be the minimum, which is that certain parts of the house are to be reserved for the religious and may not be entered by one of the opposite sex without a just and reasonable cause in the judgment of the superior. Such parts should be determined or approved by a higher superior or the general chapter. The present canon wisely enjoins, "A part of the religious house shall always be reserved to the religious alone." This reasonable privacy has not always been observed. The second paragraph states that a stricter cloister is to be observed in monasteries of men or women directed to the contemplative life.

§ 3. *Monasteries of Nuns.* When these are completely ordered to the contemplative life, they must observe papal cloister according to the norms enacted by the Apostolic See. If they have an apostolic work, they are to observe a cloister adapted to their character and defined in the constitutions, which therefore has been called constitutional cloister. These are classified in the canon merely as "other monasteries."

§ 4. *Faculties of the Diocesan Bishop*. The diocesan bishop has the faculty, for a just reason, of entering the cloister of monasteries of nuns located in his diocese, and of permitting for a serious reason and with the agreement of the superioress, that others may be admitted into the cloister and that the nuns may go out of it for the time truly necessary.

CHAPTER VII

THE EVANGELICAL COUNSELS

668. *Evangelical Counsels.* Canon 668 contains norms in relation only to religious poverty, but a canonical commentary on religious should not omit the other two evangelical counsels. The purpose of the three evangelical counsels in general was explained above under can. 598, § 1.

Definition and Purpose of Religious Chastity. The purpose of chastity is the exclusion of the divided heart in order that one may give his total love to God in Christ our Lord. In its object this religious chastity is twofold, of celibacy and perfect chastity. Celibacy, in its proper sense, is not to marry. Accordingly the religious obligation forbids marriage directly and in itself, so that contracting or attempting marriage is in itself and directly contrary to religious chastity.

Religious chastity is also an obligation of perfect chastity. Its object is that of the virtue, namely, it forbids everything already forbidden to the unmarried by the sixth and ninth commandments. Hence, the religious has a twofold obligation of perfect chastity, from the virtue of chastity by the commandments and from the public vow and thus from the virtue of religion. The official definition followed by the Roman Congregations at least from the *Normae* of 1901 was: *"By the vow of chastity, religious bind themselves to a life of celibacy and, by a new obligation from the virtue of religion, to abstain from any internal or external act opposed to chastity."*

Juridical Effects. In virtue of can. 1088 of the matrimonial law, a public perpetual vow of chastity in an institute of religious life is a diriment impediment to marriage and thus, unless dispensed, invalidates marriage.

However, unless dispensed, any other vow, private or public, or other bond, whether the vow or bond is temporary or perpetual, that directly forbids the celebration of marriage, which is true only of celibacy, or indirectly forbids the celebration of marriage: 1) because this would place one in the proximate occasion of violating the vow or bond, as is true of one of virginity or perfect chastity; 2) or makes the fulfillment of the vow or bond regularly impossible, as one of virginity, perfect chastity, of receiving sacred orders, or of entering an institute of consecrated life would forbid marriage by the natural law.

Precautions. In the *Normae* of 1901 for the constitutions of congregations of Sisters and Brothers, the S.C. of Bishops and Regulars stated that the precautions with regard to this vow could be laudably incorporated into the constitutions but not excessively nor too minutely. On May 23, 1964, Paul VI affirmed: "To attain this ideal [of perfect chastity] it is necessary to practice Christian mortification with greater zeal and also to exercise custody of the senses with more diligent care. Therefore, the life of the religious should find no place for books, periodicals, or shows which are unbecoming or indecent. . . . In a world steeped in so many forms of vice, no one can really evaluate the effectiveness of the sacred ministry of one whose life is radiant with the light of chastity consecrated to God and from which he draws his strength'' (see RfR, 34 [1975], p. 55).

Definition and Purpose of the Vow of Poverty. Constitutions approved by the Holy See have uniformly defined the simple vow of poverty as *a renunciation by the religious of the right of disposing licitly of any temporal thing of monetary value without the permission of the legitimate superior.* Since a solemn vow does not differ intrinsically from a simple vow, the same definition applies to a solemn vow. Solemn vows are not even mentioned in the new canon law on religious, in which the vows are consequently simple. This would not in itself preclude an institute from adding by its proper law the effects of a solemn profession to a simple profession. This would imply the following addition to the simple vow: By the law of the institute the professed become incapable of acquiring or retaining temporal goods for themselves. Such an addition should not be made without a previous, most serious, and factual study of the efficacy of this incapacity in attaining true religious poverty.

The obligatory aspect of the vow is evidently the prohibition of a disposition without the permission of the superior. It would be most inadequate and very harmful to the religious life to hold that the mere obligation of the vow or of law exhausts religious poverty. The purpose of the religious life is the perfection of divine charity, and the proximate purpose of the three counsels is to control the principal impediments that impede the soul from complete love of God. The proximate purpose of religious poverty is to effect such a resistance to the fascination of material things that will produce a detachment from them which will free the soul to an increased love of God. Detachment here is the habitual interior state by which one uses, requests and desires material things, not for themselves, but only insofar as they are necessary or useful for life, personal sanctification, progress in that sanctification, community life and work.

Permission is a help to the attainment of detachment but no assurance of its acquisition. Permission is highly compatible with attachment to the object permitted. It should be axiomatic that religious poverty is efficacious only insofar as it effects detachment. If a religious is not striving for detachment, poverty is contributing very little to his or her religious life. The purpose of poverty is not commanded under sin, but a religious is grieviously deceived if he does not understand that his sanctification, even after profession, is placed principally in matters of counsel. Religious poverty consequently is real and effective only in the degree that it is increasing love of God in Christ, detachment from material things, and the correlative virtues of trust in divine providence, patience, meekness, humility, and the spirit of mortification.

Material Object of Religious Poverty. The Holy See defines this object as any temporal thing of monetary value. This official definition is evident, since poverty is opposed to riches in the proper sense and consequently excludes only the things by which one can be said to be rich in the proper sense of riches. The temporal thing therefore must be: a) extrinsic to man, not his life, members, organs, powers, talents or activity of body or soul, nor his graces or virtues. b) the temporal thing must be of monetary value, money or any other object that has a value in money, since by such objects alone is anyone rich in the proper sense of the word. Hence, religious poverty is not concerned with such things as honor, fame, or reputation, since none of these has a value in money. All extrinsic goods of monetary value, whether their proprietorship appertains to the religious himself, the institute, or a third party fall under the material object of the vow.

The Formal Object of Religious Poverty. This is the aspect under which the vow touches the material object. The official definition of the Holy See defines this object as the renunciation by the religious of the right of disposing licitly (of any temporal thing of monetary value) without the permission of the legitimate superior. No vow of itself deprives one of the right of the retaining or acquiring proprietorship. When it has existed, such a privation in the past proceeded from a law added to the vow. The vow of poverty concerns only acts; only the exercise, not the right of proprietorship. The sense of the definition is simply that a disposition without permission is a sin but as such is not invalid. A disposition is, in general, a proprietary act. The term includes any disposition whatever in one's own name, that is, in the manner of an owner, and a disposition in the name of another provided it redounds to one's own material advantage or utility.

The present official expression of the vow appears to put its total effect in the necessity of the permission of the superior. In the minds of many religious, the vow of poverty becomes the same as the matter of the vow of obedience. It is thought of on the same level as a disciplinary matter as, for example, the necessity of permission to make the annual retreat in a particular place or manner. The essential object of the vow is to live without proprietorship (*sine proprio*), to use nothing as one's own, to have the mere factual use, not the proprietorship of the temporal things that the religious uses (*Nemini licet ulla re tamquam propria uti*).

It is presumed that all religious, not merely the solemnly professed (who own nothing), but also of simple vows (who should be forbidden by their own proper law to use personal property or income for themselves) will live from the goods of the institute. The permission of the superior is a concession of the mere dependent and revocable use of fact, not of the proprietorship, of an object. The poverty of a religious is essentially and primarily that of the vow, and by the vow the religious owns nothing of what he uses. His poverty is very extensive because he has no proprietorship of anything that he lives on or uses in life. The following is my attempt at a proposed new definition. *By the vow of poverty a religious is obliged to a life without proprietorship in the use and disposition of material things of monetary value, which he receives through the dependent and always revocable grant of a superior.* The vow requires the authorization of the legitimate superior also for any disposition of one's own property.

The following acts are included under the term of disposition in the official definition above.

a) *Acquisition* (acceptance of a gift, purchase, receiving a loan). Permission may readily be presumed for accepting a gift useful to the house and ordinarily there is general or at least tacit permission for the members to lend and borrow among themselves things that are in frequent use.

b) *Use or Usufruct.* This is the right of the use or of receiving the returns on property. Therefore, use beyond the limits permitted by a superior is a violation of the vow.

c) *Proprietary Possession.* Mere possession is not a proprietary act; for example, the custodian of a baggage room possesses one's luggage but not in the manner of a proprietor. Proprietary possession, as an owner, is obviously against the vow; for example, secreting an object that was acquired with permission lest it be taken by the superior.

d) *Alienation* (selling, giving away, giving a loan, exchanging objects, renunciation of a right already acquired to a temporal good). The vow therefore forbids, without the authorization of the superior, the renunciation of an inheritance or legacy. The vow does not forbid a religious to refuse a personal gift made to himself because this is not a disposition but a refusal to make a disposition, that is, an acquisition. The vow and justice forbid a religious to renounce without permission a property right already acquired for his institute, for example, to renounce a salary due for his work.

e) *Exchanging*. Morally speaking, the exchanging of objects can fail to be a proprietary act when the objects exchanged are of the same value and utility. Even if this is not true, an exchange without permission among the members of the same house will often have little guilt, since the proprietorship remains in the house and only the use is interchanged. Furthermore, a superior is presumed to be not so unwilling with regard to such an exchange.

f) *Negligence*. Negligence in the use of objects is against the vow, for example, to wear out through negligence in six months clothing that should have lasted a year. Such use is not dependent but that of a proprietor.

g) *Dispositions Made in the Name of Another*. This is to act as the agent of another. For example, if an extern gives money to a religious to be distributed to the poor, whether these are determined by the giver or to be determined by the religious, the distribution of such money without permission is not against the vow, since the disposition is not proprietary nor does it in any way enrich the religious. But a similar disposition redounding to the material utility or advantage of the religious is against the vow, whose nature is to make the religious dependent in the disposition of material things for himself. For example, an extern presents a radio, typewriter, automobile, and so forth, to a religious and says: "You do not own this; it is mine and remains mine; you have not even the strict right of using but merely the dependent use of fact, since I can always recall the object at any moment. You are always using it in my name." It is a disposition in the name of another but to one's own material advantage or utility.

h) *Mere Administration*. This in itself is only the care of property, not the exercise of proprietorship nor the obtaining of material advantage for the religious, and does not fall under the vow. Furthermore, if only the vow is considered, the superior could give permission for any proprietary act that the administration might occasion. However, can. 668, § 1 absolutely forbids a religious to administer his own property, and can. 285, § 4 prohibits a religious to administer property belonging to lay people without the permission of his own ordinary.

Authorization or Permission of the Legitimate Superior Renders a Disposition Licit. The vow of poverty forbids any disposition described above that is independent; it forbids no such disposition that is dependent. If only the express wording of the vow is considered, the superior may give permission for temporal goods of any quantity or quality. The vow says nothing expressly about quantity or quality. A disposition becomes dependent by the authorization of the legitimate superior, who is the one possessing the authority to give the particular permission. Authorization merely makes the disposition licit from its object; it does not of itself exclude sin from the circumstances or the subjective motive. Authorization does not give proprietorship; it does not make the religious the owner of the object. The religious has the mere dependent use of fact, which can always be revoked at the mere will of the superior.

Kinds of Permission. Express permission is given by a positive act of the superior. It can be explicit, which is given formally, directly, in explicit language; for example, I give you permission for this watch. Implicit permission is not expressed itself but is contained in another permission that is explicitly given; for example, the permission granted for a journey implicitly contains the permission to make the expenses necessary for the journey.

Tacit permission is not positively expressed but from external indications is legitimately deduced to exist. It is had when the superior is conscious of what is being done and remains silent when he could readily manifest opposition. Tacit permission is given by the silence of the superior whose duty is to oppose the action if he does not approve of it. An example of such a permission is had when something is done customarily in the community without the express permission of the superior and, although the act of itself demands permission, the superior is conscious of this usage but remains silent.

Presumed permission is not obtained by an act of the superior's will but is contained in the habitual will of a superior. This permission exists if it is impossible or possible only with serious difficulty, in proportion to the gravity of the disposition, to approach the superior, and it is at least probable that he would approve both the disposition and that this be done in the particular circumstances without express permission. The religious in these circumstances has real permission because he is acting with dependence on the will of his superior. Presumed permission does not exist if it is certain that the superior would disapprove of either the disposition or the doing of it without express permission.

After permission has been presumed, the vow of poverty does not oblige the member to inform the superior of the presumed permission. If such a notification is commanded by the proper law or customs, it is an obligation of either of these but not of the vow. This principle is evident from the fact that a permission given later cannot make a previous act licit.

Permission may be special, which is granted for a particular act or determined case, or general, which is granted for several cases, generally, but without being equivalent to a general dispensation from the vow.

It is possible for a superior to refuse a permission unreasonably and illicitly; for example, the refusal of something to which the religious has a right from the natural law or the proper law of the institute, such as really necessary medicines. The religious is to appeal to a higher superior. If this is impossible or inefficacious, ordinarily he should abstain from acting. However, in real necessity, the member has either presumed permission or permission from the natural or proper law, and he may obtain from externs things necessary with regard to food, clothing, and medicines according to the standard of the institute in these matters. Scandal is to be avoided, and it is evident that this case is frequently one of self-delusion.

Other Aspects of the Vow. The constitutions, directory, customs, or decrees of the general chapter may restrict some permissions to higher superiors; otherwise the local superior is competent. He has only the authority given by the proper law or customs over a visiting member of the same institute. Since no damage is caused by a violation of the vow, there is neither coalescence of different violations nor an obligation of restitution. If these do exist, they are due to the fact that justice also was violated in the act, and they are to be restricted to the act inasmuch as it is a violation of justice. Coalescence in an improper sense is verified when smaller amounts are retained until a certainly serious sum is reached. The mere intention of doing this is a serious sin against the vow.

Only external acts fall under the vow because these alone can constitute a disposition of a temporal thing. Merely interior acts can be against the vow because of the general principle that regulates such acts, which is that they are of the same moral and theological species as their object. For example, the deliberate desire to make an independent disposition notwithstanding the vow is a sin against the vow and mortal or venial according to the matter.

There is per se one malice in a violation of the vow, that contrary to the vow and thus to the virtue of religion. An independent disposition is forbidden only by the vow of poverty, not also by a law as in a violation of chastity. Accidentally there can be a multiple malice. The usual added malice is that against justice; for example, by an independent disposition of the property of the religious house, province or institute.

The sum required for a serious violation of the vow of poverty is an old question to which no satisfactory answer has been given. The following norms are probable, at least as a moral estimate of the sum required and not necessarily because of a similarity with the norms for a violation of justice. These probable norms are the absolute sum for a violation of justice, which is the highest. What may be called a fixed relative norm for the same violation, is that which would be about one half of the absolute sum. The final norm is that of a notable disposition above the state or level of poverty, which would be about one-third the absolute sum. These norms vary with the actual value of money. In one computation, the 1939 dollar was said to be worth fifteen cents in 1982.

Virtue and Spirit of Poverty. With several authors of moral theology works, it can be said that there is no specific virtue of poverty. The object of a virtue must be good in itself. Neither the lack of nor the possession of riches is good or evil in itself but is morally indifferent. What is called the virtue of poverty is a collection of virtues; for example, patience and humility, which appertain respectively to the cardinal virtues of fortitude and temperance. Religious poverty is obviously an exercise of the virtue of religion by reason of the vow. All of these virtues, including that of religion, whose immediate object is not God but the worship due to God, are infused moral, not theological, virtues. Religion is the highest of the moral virtues (see Royo Marin, *Teologia della perfezione cristiana*, no. 284).

The *theological* virtues, faith, hope, and charity, have God as their immediate object and a divine attribute as their motive. For example, by faith I assent into the existence of the Trinity because of the infinite knowledge and truthfulness of God. The theological virtues therefore refer immediately to God in their object and motive.

In the *moral* virtues God is not the immediate object and motive. These virtues are a means tending toward God, toward our supernatural end. The theological virtues are concerned with our last end, God. In the theological virtues, the immediate object is God; in the moral virtues, a good act. In the former, the motive is a divine attribute; in the latter, the moral uprightness of the act. "The infused moral virtues, as supernatural faculties, not only tend, as it were connaturally, to remove the impediments to union with God by their supernatural motive but also elevate the faculties of the soul positively and in a certain way render them inclined to the exercise of the theological virtues" (see Benigar, *Compendium theologiae spiritualis*, p. 79).

All of this coincides with the purpose of the evangelical counsels in the consecrated life, which is to control the principal obstacles to the striving for the perfection of the infused theological virtue of charity. The immediate purpose of religious poverty is the control of the fascination for material things, which can impede and exclude this perfection of love (see RfR, 35 [1976], 735-9).

In two documents of the Holy See, the *Statutes for Extern Sisters*, of 1931, and the *Norms for Diocesan Missionary Congregations*, of 1940, identical definitions are given of what the former terms the "spirit" (no.

65) and the latter the "virtue" (no. 57) of poverty: "The spirit [virtue] of poverty implies also that the sisters put off all inordinate affection for temporal things and bear their privation, if it occurs, with a cheerful and courageous mind" (see RfR, 37 [1978], 745-6).

Apostolic Character of Poverty. There is no doubt that the personal and community poverty of a religious institute should have an apostolic effect, be an image, a sign that leads others to the proper evaluation of, desire for, and use of the material things of life. Whether the apostolate in itself falls directly under religious poverty is a question that I have not seen nor heard proposed but it merits reflection and not mere presumption. Education at all levels, hospitals, nursing and other homes for the aged, care of disturbed boys and girls, institutions for the orphaned and handicapped, assistance in the parish ministry, counseling, and the care of dependent children are the common fields of apostolic religious in general.

I think I am fair in taking a hospital or a college as an example regarding poverty. I do not believe that religious erect, equip and maintain a hospital or college with poverty as their guide. They have one evident norm: what is the best building and other means for the care of the sick or education, not what is poor or the poorest. Medicines, for example, are purchased for their efficacy, not because of conformity with poverty. It is true that in all these apostolates religious should avoid superfluities, extravagance, and wastefulness, but this appertains to capable management, not necessarily to religious poverty. Completely secular institutions also follow this policy. I do not therefore see that the apostolate is a direct field of the application of religious poverty. Religious have the profession of poverty; their apostolate is for others. For example, the buildings for the apostolate of religious are not primarily intended for the benefit of the religious but for the subjects of their apostolate, who do not have the profession of religious poverty (see RfR, ibid., 744-5).

Poverty of Law. The following are the matters in religious poverty that were obligations from law, not from the vow:

The incapacity of solemnly professed religious to acquire or retain the proprietorship of temporal things for themselves.

The invalidity of acts contrary to solemn vows.

The renunciation of personal property obligatory before solemn profession.

The retained right of acquisition and ownership of professed of simple vows, that is, of what has been given to them certainly as a private person. This right may be limited or taken away completely by the constitutions but this has most rarely been done in fact.

Cession of administration and disposition of the use and usufruct to be made by those actually owning property.

The making of a will.

The observance of common life in material things.

The following are the laws of can. 668 on religious poverty.

668, §§ 1-2. *Cession of Administration and Disposition of Use and Usufruct to be Made by Those Actually Owning Property*. Administration is the care of property, that is, maintaining it, keeping it in repair, investing it and securing the returns on investments. Any novice who actually owns property must before his first profession of religious temporary vows and thus in about the last month of his noviceship cede to whomever (one or many) he chooses the administration of his property. The administrator may be chosen for a determined length or for as long as one remains a member of the institute. The cession is effective at the first profession. After the first profession, exactly the same thing is to be done for any property or added property coming to the member after first profession. The cession is of obligation and in practice is made only for property actually owned at the time, even though it would not be contradictory in itself nor contrary to the canon to make it for property to be acquired in the future. The member is perfectly free in choosing the administrator. He may sign over the administration to the institute, with its consent, or to an extern. To avoid any civil difficulties, it is expedient to add a clause that the administrator may be changed at the mere will of the religious.

Disposition of the Use and Usufruct. The novices and professed are here disposing only of the use and income, not of the principal of their personal property. The circumstances given above (time of making and effectiveness, only by owners of property, simultaneous with future acquisitions) for cession of the administration apply also to the disposition. It is to be remembered that in canon law the member is perfectly free in choosing the beneficiaries of the use and usufruct. However, proper law prescribing that all or part be given to a determined beneficiary or forbidding that the income accrue to the capital, that is, proper law that takes away, restricts or defines the right is to be observed. Such provisions of proper law were most rare in the past.

Making of a Will. A will is a disposition in whole or in part of the property that one will own at death by an act that is revocable until death and effective only at death. All religious are to make a will and one that is also valid in civil law. The will is to be made at least before perpetual profession. It may be made previously if the member is capable of making a will valid according to civil law. The will is to be made even if one does not actually own property. It is then made only for property that the individual will acquire in the future and own at the time of his death.

Changes. Any change in the cession of administration, disposition of the use and usufruct, and of the will requires a just reason and the permission of the superior competent according to proper law, which should assign this duty to the immediate higher superior. He and his staff are more likely to be conversant with such matters than a minor local superior. The meaning with regard to a will is a real change; that is, in the beneficiaries. It is not a change to interpret the will, to put it in a better and clearer form, to add a disposition with regard to property recently acquired, or to substitute a beneficiary for one who has died. This can. 668, § 2 adds that the permission of the same superior is necessary for a member to place "any act in the matter of temporal goods." This is true but it is the direct obligation of the religious vow of poverty. One wonders therefore why it was placed here and presumably also as an obligation of law.

668, § 3. *Limitation of the Right of Acquisition.* This limitation is a universal law and thus applies to all religious institutes. The religious acquires for his institute whatever comes to him (1) "by his activity." The canon is absolute and is to be understood absolutely. Therefore, it does not matter whether the activity, labor or work is intellectual or physical, ordinary or extraordinary, within or outside the scope of his institute. (2) "with respect to his institute." This clause includes anything the religious receives for his institute, because the intention of the donor is then to give to the institute, not to the religious, and anything he receives when the motive of the giver is the fact that he is a religious or a religious of the particular institute.

The presumption is that gifts from relatives and all inheritances and legacies are made to the religious as a private person but all other gifts are made to him as a religious. (3) "in any way as a pension, assistance or insurance . . . unless the contrary is established in proper law." This section therefore includes a pension from any source; for example, a former employer or a government, as also any form of old age assistance, and any insurance.

§ 4. *The "Nature" of an Institute Demands the Renunciation of All Personal Property*. It is not specified in the canon what institutes are here intended, even though the distinction of "nature" is new, nor is there otherwise any certainty about the institutes intended. I presume that the religious in all cases may renounce his then owned property in favor of whomever, one or many, he individually and voluntarily chooses because he is then the owner of the property. The professed of temporary vows of these institutes are to renounce (give) all the property they presently own in favor of whomever, one or many, they choose, and they are to renounce in favor of their institute all property to be acquired in the future. The latter can be said to follow from § 5.

This renunciation is to be done in a form valid, as far as possible, also in civil law, before perpetual profession but effective only from the emission of this profession. This same form shall be used by the professed of perpetual vows of any other religious institute who, with the permission of the general superior, are voluntarily renouncing according to proper law their goods wholly or partially. In the first case, the full renunciation is obligatory from the nature of the institute; in the second case, the full or partial renunciation is voluntary, i.e., the extent of a voluntary renunciation depends on the intention and the expression of his or her intention by the one renouncing the property. This renunciation may be of part of his temporal possessions, of all of them, and of the right to acquire temporal possessions in the future.

§ 5. *Effects of the Obligatory Renunciation.* The effect of the full renunciation obligatory from the nature of an institute is that the religious loses the capacity of acquiring and retaining ownership of temporal goods for himself. Therefore, all proprietary acts that he thereafter places without permission are not only illicit, because they are against the vow, but also invalid, because he is necessarily disposing of property that is not his own. The property that he acquires in the future will be owned by the institute, province or house according to the norm of proper law.

Voluntary Renunciation and Proper Law. For a voluntary renunciation, proper law may demand a longer time, e.g., ten years of perpetual vows. It is obvious that the permission should not be given to religious of unstable vocation. The general superior is to strive to learn of any personal or family circumstances that would render the granting of the permission imprudent. All prescripts of proper law are evidently also to be observed, e.g., that the general superior have the consultative or deliberative vote of his or her council to give the permission for a voluntary renunciation.

Common Life in Material Things. This important matter, with the exception of the generalities on the limit of material things in can. 600, is not mentioned in the proposed canons, but there should be legislation on it in the proper law of each religious institute. The 1917 code, in can. 594, was opposed to the habitual possession of money by individual religious, which I believe should now be restricted in such practices as the personal budget to money for incidental expenses (see RfR, 33 [1974], 966-9). The same canon contained the obligation that the material necessities of a religious were at least ordinarily and habitually to be supplied by the institute and to be received from the institute by the religious. The canon did not forbid religious from receiving gifts for their personal use provided this was done with permission; the proprietorship appertained to the institute; in quantity, quality, and value the thing did not exceed what would have been given by the institute; and that this was done only infrequently, occasionally, and almost accidentally.

By the profession or state of poverty is meant the limit in quantity, quality, and value of material things that each institute permits for the use of its religious. This limit is to be ascertained from an express declaration of the proper law or more frequently from the legitimate customs and traditions of the particular institute. Can. 594, § 3 obliged superiors immediately in conscience to provide the material necessities of the religious according to this limit and not to exceed it in furnishing their necessities. This canon of the 1917 code likewise obliged all religious immediately in conscience not to exceed this limit in their requests and use of material things. Things above this limit are styled as superfluities. It was therefore evident that there was a sin against this law in granting, requesting, or using superfluities. At least for apostolic institutes, the profession or state of poverty should be that of simplicity, which is the exclusion of the luxurious, extravagant, and superfluous, and the living of an economical and careful life in material things (see RfR, 37 [1978], 742-4).

The consequence of the preceding paragraph is a moral uniformity among the religious of any particular institute in material things. This uniformity admits reasonable diversity; for example, because of sickness a religious may be given special medicines, treatments and food, a religious studying science may need expensive instruments, those in studies or various fields of teaching or writing may need more books, and so forth. It is clear that a lack of generosity by superiors readily leads to violations of the vow and especially of common life. It is equally evident that a disregard of this paragraph by superiors and members will not leave the peace and harmony of the community untroubled.

Religious Obedience. As stated in the purpose of the evangelical counsels under can. 601, the purpose of obedience is to control the excessive love of self, or pride. Obedience is considered the greatest of the religious vows simply because it is to control the greatest obstacle to the perfection of divine love lived in Christ our Lord. The clearest Scriptural expression of this purpose is found in St. Paul, "he humbled himself becoming obedient to death, even to the death on a cross" (Ph 2:8). The logic of the vows demands this purpose since the purpose of chastity and poverty is to control the other principal obstacles to such charity, the divided heart and the fascination of material possessions.

Obedience is not in the religious life merely for itself nor as the supreme virtue of the Christian or religious life, but as the principal negative means to the perfection of divine charity. Obedience, as the continuous subjection to another in so many aspects of life, leads to the constant practice of faith and humility and thus aids the complete gift of self to love of God. Concretely this love is lived personally in living Christ, who said of himself, "Because I came down from heaven not to do my own will but the will of him that sent me" (Jn 6:38).

The essence of the obedience of a religious is as a religious, on matters therefore concerning the religious life, which is usually expressed as "according to the vows and constitutions." The vow of obedience is defined: *by the vow of obedience religious consecrate to God their own will and oblige themselves from the virtue of religion to obey the commands of their lawful superior in everything that directly or indirectly concerns the observance of the vows, the Rule, if the institute has a Rule, and the constitutions* (see no. 132 of the *Normae* of 1901).

Obedience is not intended to defeat or lessen sound human development. This would be contrary to the clear teaching of Vatican II. "The gospel . . . constantly advises that all human talents be employed in God's service and men's . . . " (GES, no. 41). "Formation for the apostolate means a certain human and well-rounded formation adapted to the natural abilities and circumstances of each lay person" (AA, no. 29). The Holy See had already maintained in preconciliar documents that personal sanctification must be based on a solid foundation of natural virtue and cultured refinement, and that nothing capable of perfecting body and mind and of fully developing all natural virtues should be neglected.

Vatican II affirmed that the observance of the counsels: "does not detract from a genuine development of the human person. Rather by its very nature it is most beneficial to that development" (LG, no. 46). The council urged superiors to lead the members to an active and responsible obedience, to serve and not dominate them, and that councils and chapters should express the fact that all members have a share in the welfare of the whole community and a responsibility for it (PC, no. 14).

"To govern is to serve, not to dominate," became an early post-conciliar axiom. This is true, but to serve others should be verified in all men and women as a demand of the virtue of charity. The danger of a superior seems to me rather that of smothering the community and the persons of its members, in being the center and focus of practically everything, or supervising, taking over, leading, assisting and directing when these are neither necessary nor useful. An equal danger is the lack of authority and firmness when these are clearly demanded. Many serious community and personal problems have developed even to an intolerable degree through the weakness of superiors. The superior should act in such a way that he fosters and does not impede the maturity and initiative of the members, and in these their personality development is sufficiently contained.

The mature religious must have spiritual and apostolic initiative, be able to think for himself, to get new ideas, at least ordinarily to direct his own spiritual life. He must be personally mature, have confidence in his own judgment, a willingness to make decisions and to persevere in them, and a habitual fearlessness in facing reality and unpleasant facts without rationalization or self-pity.

He does not think he is perfect, the center of all things; neither is he over-dependent on others. He is mature in work, dependable, reliable, efficient, persevering; he gives more than the job demands; he can face and handle his own problems of work. He is emotionally mature. His emotional reactions are habitually adult. He is not ruled by imagination or feeling, does not live a life of fantasy, nor is he frequently disturbed by trifles; he does not pout or sulk, make a scene or blow up; he seldom if ever has an emotional storm; and he is not a mendicant of attention or publicity. He understands defects without condoning them or being scandalized by them, and is not disillusioned by the conduct of others.

He does not fall into adolescent crushes nor allow himself affections that are proper to those who can marry. He has the ability to work and cooperate with others, to be an individual and part of an organization; he is reasonably ambitious but not at the expense of others nor with the desire to excel others. He has so formed himself that he has a professional skill that will enable him to have a satisfactory life of work. He is mature in community life. He takes more than his share of the common burdens; he does things for the community. He does not merely receive from others nor shirk his duties, and much less is he childishly unconscious of them. In a word, the religious is a man or a woman, not a child or an adolescent.

The office of a superior requires outstanding human ability, prudence and tact. The difficulty in finding a sufficient number of competent superiors is a surprisingly unrealized problem in institutes of religious life. Many think the difficulty is that competent superiors have not been appointed. The problem is finding competence, not ignoring it.

1. *Remote Matter of the Vow.* This is what can be made the matter of an obligation of the vow. The remote matter is restricted to the material execution of what is directly or indirectly contained in the other vows, the Rule, and the constitutions: directly is anything explicitly contained in these sources, for example, to go to an assigned house; indirectly or implicitly, is something necessary or very useful for the observance of anything explicitly contained in the same sources. Material execution, that is, the obligation of the vow extends only to the mere material or nude execution of what is commanded, since the religious promises merely to obey, not to obey from any particular motive.

In a doubt as to whether a command is sinful or according to the vows, Rule, or constitutions, the member is obliged to obey. The presumption favors the superior and he is not to be deprived of his right to command unless he certainly exceeds this authority. The member can also form his conscience to obey such a command. This presumption does not exist if the power of the superior to command in any complete line of conduct is seriously doubtful. There is then no obligation to obey, as stated below regarding merely interior acts. A religious by his incorporation into the institute through profession is subject to the authority of his institute. He is thus obliged to obey the proper laws and the commands of superiors as a member of the institute and from the virtue of obedience, even though these do not ordinarily oblige in conscience. Consequently, the *Normae* of 1901, no. 134, as other typical constitutions published by the Holy See, states, "A sister is obliged from the virtue of obedience to fulfill the dispositions of the constitutions and of superiors."

No obligation exists to obey a command that is certainly sinful or certainly against the vows, Rule, or constitutions. However, a superior who has the power and a legitimate reason for a dispensation, may give a dispensation and a command of the vow to observe it. There is no obligation to obey a command above the same sources; for example, of austerities in no way contained in these sources, such as always to sleep on the floor, never to eat meat, to rise daily at midnight for two hours of prayer. Religious are also not obliged to obey a precept of the vow to an act that implies serious loss, harm, or danger, since as in human law so also the precept of a superior does not oblige in such cases. The obligation does exist if such acts are contained in the purpose or constitutions of an institute. No obligation is had to obey things certainly outside or beneath the same sources, that is, things that are certainly idle, useless, or lax.

Interior acts necessary for an external act, for example, that priests celebrate Mass for a determined intention, may certainly be commanded in virtue of the vow, as the Sacred Congregation for Religious replied (AAS, 6 [1914], 231). External acts and circumstances necessary for interior acts may also be commanded by reason of the vow; for example, with regard to such acts as meditation or examen of conscience, it is certain that the superior may give a precept of the vow to abstain from all external acts and to be in a place and in circumstances where such interior acts can be performed. The command would then extend only to external actions.

Many authors affirm that superiors may command merely interior acts in virtue of the vow, because Christian spirituality consists principally in such acts and hence the power of superiors is contained in the purpose and nature of the religious life. Several authors hold that such a command may be given for merely interior acts prescribed by the Rule or constitutions, such as meditation or examen, because obedience is vowed according to these. Other authors simply deny this power to superiors. Their argument is that human government is restricted to human relations, and these are confined to external acts. The practical conclusion is that a member is not obliged to obey a command of the vow to a merely interior act. The presumption of the possession of authority does not reasonably favor the superior when his power is doubtful with regard to the entire species of the acts in question.

2. *Proximate Matter of the Vow.* The proximate matter of the vow, that which brings the obligation of the vow into actual existence, demands at least the strict command of a lawful superior. A strict command is the express imposition of an obligation immediately in conscience, immediately under sin, to do something, to omit something, or to fulfill a punishment. The superior must manifest clearly the intention of obliging in conscience, for example, "I command, order, forbid you in conscience." A strict command is not the mere good pleasure of a superior (It would please me), a desire (I would like), a counsel (It would be better), mere firm will (That is not to be done), an admonition (Do not do that), or a merely penal precept, which is a precept obliging only under a punishment for its non-observance. The superior may oblige under mortal or venial sin in serious matter but only under venial sin in light matter because such matter does not admit a grave obligation.

a) *Strict Precept or Strict Precept in Virtue of the Vow?* To produce the obligation of the vow of obedience, is a strict command sufficient or is there required a strict command in virtue of the vow of obedience? If the latter, the superior must add to the strict command one of the clauses in use in the particular institute for manifesting a command in virtue of the vow, for example, "in virtue of holy obedience." This clause may be added explicitly or implicitly, that is, in other words. The answer depends on the way the vow is understood in the particular institute, because obedience is vowed according to the Rule and constitutions. If understood in the former sense, every strict command produces the obligation of the vow. In these institutes clauses such as "in virtue of holy obedience" manifest a command of the vow under serious sin.

In at least practically all lay institutes and in many clerical institutes, the vow is understood in the second sense; and this is the practice of the Holy See in approving the constitutions of nuns, sisters, and brothers. Therefore, in these institutes the determined clauses in use in the particular institute must be employed to produce any obligation of the vow of obedience. The clauses most usually found in practice are: "in virtue or in the name of holy obedience," "under formal precept," "in virtue or in the name of our Lord Jesus Christ," "in virtue or in the name of the Holy Spirit," "in virtue or in the name of God," "in virtue or in the name of the vow of obedience," "under pain of serious sin," and "under pain of divine judgment."

b) *Rule, Constitutions and the Vow of Obedience*. According to the practice of the Holy See in approving constitutions, the Rule and the constitutions do not of themselves in fact oblige from the vow of obedience, as is explicitly stated in no. 133 of the *Normae* of 1901. Furthermore, since the Rule and constitutions in general do not oblige immediately under sin, it is evident that they cannot oblige in virtue of the vow of obedience because the latter always produces an obligation immediately under sin. A precept in virtue of the vow of obedience may be given not only by the particular act of a superior but may also be contained in a permanent manner in the constitutions. Therefore, some articles of constitutions that do not in general oblige immediately under sin or from the vow may be precepts given expressly in virtue of the vow of obedience. Such precepts are in fact practically never found in the constitutions of lay institutes. If a Rule or constitutions oblige immediately under sin, the obligation is also as a precept of the vow only if this is the understanding of the vow in the particular institute. The reason is again that obedience is vowed according to the Rule and constitutions.

c) *Grave Matter Required?* The vow of obedience in itself admits an obligation in either grave or light matter and under either mortal or venial sin. However, most constitutions of lay institutes were based on the *Normae* of 1901. Even though several authors (Bastien, no. 582, 4; Lanslots, no. 220; Wernz-Vidal, *De religiosis*, no. 363, note 100) hold the contrary doctrine, it would be most difficult to admit an obligation under venial sin in these norms. They state explicitly that a religious is obliged to obey by reason of the vow only when commanded in virtue of holy obedience or by a similar formula (no. 135); they enact that such precepts are to be given only rarely, cautiously, in writing or at least in the presence of two witnesses (no. 136); and command that local superiors, especially of small houses, refrain from giving such precepts (no. 137).

In 1931 the Sacred Congregation for Religious repeated the same prescriptions in nos. 58-9 of the *Statutes for Extern Sisters*, and the S.C. for the Propagation of the Faith almost the same in no. 68 of the norms destined for diocesan missionary congregations. Constitutions that contain prescriptions such as those above permit a precept in virtue of the vow to be given only in grave matter and under mortal sin. It seems evident that other institutes should follow this long practice of the Holy See as a directive norm. The actual usage of religious institutes is to give precepts in virtue of the vow only in matters that are most serious and usually also scandalous; for example, to break off dangerous and scandalous relations with persons of the other sex.

3. *Formalities Recommended.* The formalities recommended to lay institutes by the Holy See for giving a precept in virtue of the vow were stated in the preceding paragraph. They should be followed as a directive norm also by other institutes. A written precept is preferable because it furnishes a more ready proof if later the formalities of a dismissal are begun.

4. *The Lawful Superior.* A command in virtue of the vow can obviously be given only by a superior who has the authority to do so. All superiors possess authority according to the constitutions and some of pontifical clerical institutes have also ecclesiastical jurisdiction. By his vow of obedience, the religious does not create the authority that the

superior already possesses from canon law and the constitutions but the latter merely acquires another title for the exercise of this same authority. A command in virtue of the vow may be imposed by either the usual authority or jurisdiction. However, since ecclesiastical jurisdiction is exercised only for such matters as the enacting of laws, dispensing from them, inflicting canonical punishments and granting jurisdiction to confessors, it is evident that precepts in virtue of the vow of obedience are practically always given from the usual authority also in pontifical clerical institutes.

Those competent to give such a precept are the Roman Pontiff, an ecumenical council and the SCRSI. Among internal authorities, this competency appertains to the general chapter, as also the provincial chapter but only if such a power is given to it by the constitutions; higher superiors and consequently the general and provincial superiors in centralized institutes; local superiors according to the constitutions, but not the local assistant unless such a power is given to the latter by the constitutions or by delegation from a competent superior, who may delegate another to give a precept in virtue of the vow of obedience. In the constitutions of sisters and brothers at times the local superior is clearly denied the power of giving a command in virtue of the vow or forbidden to give such a precept (see *Normae* of 1901, no. 137), or his power is restricted to an urgent case, not infrequently with the explicit obligation of immediately notifying the higher superior. At least the local major superior of an autonomous monastery or house may also give a precept in virtue of the vow.

5. *Number of Sins in a Violation of a Command of the Vow.* It is usually stated that such a violation has a twofold malice in itself, a violation of the vow and also of the virtue of obedience by the obligation to obey contracted through religious profession, by which one becomes a member of the institute and subject to its authority. It is, however, solidly probable that there is only one malice, that against the vow and thus the virtue of religion. Some explain this by stating that the obligation from the vow and incorporation into the institute are here considered as one. It is preferable to hold that the superior is here employing the title

from the vow of obedience and there is no reason to maintain that he is also using the title from incorporation, unless he intends this and externally expresses such an intention.

6. *Merit of the Vow of Obedience.* Since the obligation of the vow is so rarely imposed, the question naturally arises whether a religious ever obtains the merit of the vow of obedience. The subjective intention of the religious determines the merit; and the presumption is that a religious in all his obedience, in all subjection to any type of will of his superior, obeys because of his vow of obedience, unless he positively excludes this motive, and thus acquires the merit of the vow.

7. *Representation and Recourse.* In matters of at least some importance, when solid reasons exist against a command or directive of a superior, a member may represent such reasons to the superior, since religious obedience is a rational obligation. A member may also recur to a higher superior against a decision of a lower superior for the same kind of reasons. A recourse does not suspend the decision or directive of the lower superior, which is to be obeyed while the recourse is pending.

8. *Necessary and Perfect Obedience.* Necessary obedience of the vow is confined to the material observance of a strict precept of the vow, as explained above; perfect obedience of the vow is that which is not strictly commanded. There is a field of both obligation and counsel in the religious vow of obedience, and these two we shall hereafter designate as necessary and perfect obedience. The distinction is of great practical moment. It is evident that very few religious will ever receive a precept in virtue of the vow, and consequently obedience will not be operative in the life of a religious unless he is striving habitually for at least an appreciable degree of perfect obedience. Necessary and perfect obedience of the vow are distinguished as follows.

a) *Extension.* Necessary obedience does not go beyond the things that are a strict command of the vow; perfect obedience of the vow includes also the mere good pleasure, desires, counsels, mere firm will, admonitions, and merely penal precepts, all even anticipated, of a superior.

b) *Execution.* Necessary obedience is restricted to the material execution of the thing commanded; perfect obedience extends to the promptness, alacrity, thoroughness, courage, perseverance, and constancy, without excuse, complaint, or criticism, in carrying out the will of the superior.

c) *Interior Dispositions*. Necessary obedience is limited to the material execution of the thing commanded. In perfect obedience, the religious conforms his will by doing willingly what he was directed. The conformity of wills requires that the member do willingly what the superior wishes and excludes consent to inclinations opposed to his will. Approval of the thing commanded and esteem and liking for the superior can help but cannot be the primary motive of obedience.

The authority of all religious superiors is derived from canon law, the law of the Roman Pontiff, and from the constitutions, which are effective in virtue of the authorization of the Holy See or of the diocesan bishop in diocesan institutes. Therefore, the authority of religious superiors is mediately from God through the Roman Pontiff and diocesan bishops. Only by this fact of the possession of authority mediately from God is the will of the superior the will of God, and the superior the representative of and one who holds the place of God, and evidently not because he is omniscient, infallible, or impeccable.

Interior conformity with the superior causes no difficulty when the thing ordered or counseled by the superior appears to be the best, the most reasonable, prudent, useful, and profitable. If it is doubtfully such, the religious by perfect obedience turns to the reasons for rather than those against the directive of the superior; he controls the influence of the passions—that is, pride, anger, sensuality, sloth—which tend to turn the judgment against the directive of the superior.

He is guided also by the consciousness that the superior has the grace of state and ordinarily more sources of knowledge and a wider outlook than a member. If what is ordered is evidently not the best, the religious cannot think that such a thing is in itself the best. Even here, however, by perfect obedience he conforms his mind to that of the superior extrinsically; that is, this thing less perfect in itself is in these circumstances the more perfect thing because it is the will of God for him by reason of the order of the superior.

CHAPTER VIII

OTHER OBLIGATIONS OF RELIGIOUS INSTITUTES AND MEMBERS

669, § 1. *Wearing of Religious Habit Obligatory.* The habit is to be worn by religious as a sign of their consecration and testimony of their poverty. Religious are obliged to wear the habit; the form of the habit is left to the proper law of the institute but it obviously must always be a habit, traditional or modified. The habit, as one of the things approved by the Holy See, could be neither changed nor abolished by a particular institute, pontifical or diocesan, without the permission of the Holy See. This doctrine was in peaceful possession before Vatican II, when also no one even thought of the abolition of the habit.

Vatican II, in *Perfectae caritatis*, no. 17, said merely that the habit of men or women could be modified and, if unsuitable, should be modified. It said nothing whatever about the abolition of the habit. A permission to change was not a permission to abolish. The SCRSI has constantly repeated: change, yes; abolition, no. The sacred congregation, in its repeated statement of this principle, was not making a new law but merely declaring the clear objective sense of Vatican II, to which it referred with equal constancy.

The constitutions, general chapter, or a higher superior may permit the wearing of becoming secular clothes, foreign to affectation and vanity, in special circumstances, e.g., when the habit would be an obstacle to the normal exercise of a work or ministry or "some moment of recreation": "exceptions may be made, e.g., regarding sport, but the norms of common sense apply here just as well as everywhere else"; "it does not seem prudent to grant general freedom with regard to vacations, but particular occasions could be considered." The wearing of the habit is not to be left to the individual religious. The general principles of wearing the habit should be in the constitutions, the details of the habit in the directory.

§ 2. *Dress of Religious Priests and Deacons.* In his letter to the Cardinal Vicar of Rome, September 8, 1982, John Paul II affirmed that ecclesiastical dress contributed to the decorum of the priest in his external comportment, that it was a sign of the public testimony that every priest is bound to give of his identity and of his special dedication to God, and an aid in preserving the priest from any desire to hide his priesthood before men and to avoid all external signs of it. His clerical dress distinguishes him from the secular environment in which he lives. The religious habit expresses the consecration and the eschatological end of the religious life.

Religious clerics (priests and deacons) of an institute that does not have a distinctive habit assume clerical dress in the new code according to can. 284 which reads, "Clerics shall wear an appropriate ecclesiastical attire, according to the norms determined by the conference of bishops and legitimate local customs." At least a pari religious clerics who have a distinctive religious habit are held by the same law in places where the religious habit and the cassock are legitimately not worn on the street.

In his norms for the diocese of Rome, the Cardinal Vicar includes as the fifth norm: "The soutane [cassock] or the religious habit is of obligation in liturgical celebrations, in the administration of the sacraments, and in preaching. It is strongly advised in the ambient of one's own pastoral ministry." *The New Order of the Mass*, edited by J. Patino, Collegeville, MN, The Liturgical Press, 1970, states in note 81, p. 158, "The cassock is not mentioned under the alb during liturgical services. The biretta is not mentioned either." The authors thus logically conclude, "It does not seem necessary to wear it [the cassock] under the alb during liturgical services." The surplice over a cassock and a stole were mentioned in later publications of liturgical norms at least as the alternative vestments for such acts as the administration of Holy Communion outside of Mass and for exposition of the Blessed Sacrament.

In their 1967 and 1974 meetings, the National Conference of Bishops of the United States affirmed their position, "that the Roman collar and the dark black suit is the proper street attire for the clergy" (see RfR, 35 [1976], p. 76).

672. *Canons on Clerics Obligatory on Professed Religious.* These are here stated to be cann. 277, 285-87 and 289 and religious clerics also by can. 279, § 2. In pontifical lay institutes of men and women, the permission required by can. 285, § 4 may be granted by their own major superior.

277. *Perfect Chastity and Celibacy of Clerics.* The obligation of clerics is to observe perfect chastity, which is complete external and interior chastity, and not to marry. This obligation obviously extends to all religious clerics as clerics.

§§ 2-3. *Prudent Conduct.* Clerics should conduct themselves with due prudence when they associate with persons whose company can imperil the observance of continence or cause scandal to the faithful. It appertains to the diocesan bishop to establish more specific rules in this matter and to pass judgment in particular cases on the observance of this obligation.

285, § 1. Clerics must abstain from all activities which are unbecoming to their state in accordance with the prescripts of particular law. Such acts were defined in the past as those that lower or demean the clerical state. They are to be found in the particular law of dioceses, provincial councils and conferences of bishops.

§ 2. *Avoidance of Things Alien to the Clerical State.* In general these are matters somewhat unbecoming to the clerical state or that impede the clerical ministry. Usually they are secular affairs and are more precisely defined in the remaining words of the canon and in such other sources as decrees of conferences of bishops, provincial councils, and in diocesan statutes.

§ 3. *Civil Jurisdiction or Administration.* Clerics are not to assume public offices, especially those involving the exercise of civil jurisdiction or administration, e.g., that of president, governor, mayor, member of cabinet, judge, magistrate, senator or representative. Dispensations from this pontifical law appertain to the Holy See.

§ 4. *Secular Matters*. Without the permission of their own ordinary, clerics may not be managers of business affairs or of properties that belong to lay people or assume secular offices that necessitate the rendering of an account. They may not assume the guardianship of orphans and widows, be administrators or executors of wills, nor be president, treasurer, secretary, or directors of banks, even of those that are of a charitable or social type, or of other economic societies. Clerics are forbidden, without consulting the local ordinary, to assume the obligation, even with their own property, of paying a debt if the debtor himself fails to do so, or to sign promissory notes whereby the obligation to pay for an undetermined purpose is undertaken. In pontifical lay institutes of men and women, the permission may be granted by or the consultation had with the proper major superior (see can. 672 above).

286. *Business and Trading*. Business and trading signify the same thing. The general meaning is ''acts that are done exclusively, predominantly, primarily for the purpose of profit.'' The purpose of the law is to prevent clerics and religious from being involved in temporal matters unbecoming to their state and to avoid distractions from and neglect of the duties of their state. Furthermore, the danger of scandalizing others or of provoking attacks or suspicions will at times induce clerics and religious to avoid acts that are not forbidden by this canon. The practical cases usually concern religious.

The canon forbids *habitual* performance of acts of business and trading. Therefore, a single act, or such acts rarely performed, even in matter that if habitual would be serious, is not forbidden by the canon. The prohibition of the canon includes business or trading that is performed personally or through others, with the property of an individual religious or that of the house, province, or institute, for personal profit or that of others, even though the profit is destined for laudable or holy purposes. The prohibition is verified only if all of the following four conditions are present. If any one of these is not verified in the acts, it is not forbidden by the canon:

1) that the object be bought and sold;

2) that it be sold unchanged or changed by hired labor;

3) that it be sold at a price higher than the complete cost price;

4) that it be purchased with the exclusive or at least predominant and primary intention, at the time of the purchase, of selling it at a higher price.

1) The object must be purchased. Religious do not violate the law when they sell the products of their fields, grain, fruit, and vegetables. They may likewise sell wool, hides, eggs, butter, and milk produced by their herds and flocks, as well as calves, lambs, chickens, pigs, and other animals. They may do such things as making bread from the grain produced by their fields, wine from grapes produced in their vineyards. They may use hired help for all these things and sell all at a profit. They may do this also with articles received as gifts because these were not purchased by the religious.

2) Religious may purchase objects to be changed by their own labor to sell them at a profit. They may sell needlework, embroidery, vestments, and works of art produced by the religious such as paintings and sculptures; they may buy materials and make from them uniforms, habits and veils. They may purchase grain or grapes and make bread and wine from them. The same act is forbidden when the change is to be effected by paid labor, e.g., religious are forbidden to purchase grapes to be made into wine in order to sell it at a profit. Renting in law is not the same as purchasing. Therefore, it is not certainly forbidden to rent land for pasturing cattle or for cultivating, even by hired help, to sell the cattle or the crops at a profit.

Students in such places as industrial schools are not considered as hired labor, even if moderate wages are paid to them. Religious may sell for a profit the products of such students who are being trained for various trades or arts.

3) To fall under the prohibition, the object must be sold at a price

higher than the full purchase price, which includes not only the original cost but also the expenses of transportation, storage, conservation, the wages paid to hired help, and any other expenses. If no profit is made on the transaction above the complete cost, the act is not forbidden.

4) Religious may resell, even with a great but just profit, objects which were not bought with the intention of reselling at a profit, e.g., they may sell stocks and bonds which have risen in value, even though they have the intention of buying other stocks and bonds with the proceeds of the sale. They may even buy stocks and bonds with the intention of selling them if the price advances. However, they may not buy stocks or bonds with the exclusive, predominant and primary intention of selling them at a profit. In the former case the act is merely the prudent change from a good to a better investment or the prudent cessation of an investment; in the latter case the act is speculation. Religious may sell, even for profit, objects which have become useless or superfluous, e.g., furniture, materials, books, etc.

The intention of selling for a profit must be exclusive, or at least predominant or primary. The following cases are pertinent: religious buying medicines to sell to patients in hospitals or similar institutions; buying school supplies, books, pamphlets, food and drink, etc., to be sold to students of a school; buying devotional articles, rosaries, crucifixes, prayer books to be sold to students or retreatants; having a gift counter, coffee shop, cafeteria in a hospital, etc. It is evident in these and similar cases that they are to avoid the appearance of being in business or of seeking profit. The purpose in all such cases is the convenience, utility, necessity of the students, patients, etc. Since the purpose is not exclusively nor predominantly profit, these acts are not forbidden. The articles may be sold at the current retail price. The action is not illicit and there is no obligation from this canon of using the profit to benefit the students, etc., in a way that would not otherwise be due to them.

Religious may sell at the current and just price an object that was purchased at a reduced price when the cause of the reduction was a favor or gift to the religious. The profit is then made not on a purchased object but a gift.

Religious may operate a printing plant: (1) if the work is carried on by the religious themselves or the members of their household, even if a few outsiders are hired to help; (2) it is also licit to use paid employees to run the plant if it prints only works composed by the religious themselves. The latter case is illicit if the plant prints books written by externs. However, even this would be licit if the printing consists of religious reviews, magazines, journals, and other forms of religious literature destined for the spread of the faith and school books that cannot be obtained elsewhere.

It is evident that the canon also includes trading in currency, as when the money of one country is exchanged for that of another with the exclusive or predominant purpose of profit.

". . . except with the permission of legitimate ecclesiastical authority." Since the norm is a canon, the legitimate authority that may permit religious to exercise business or trading is the Holy See. The same reservation to the Holy See is found in *De Episcoporum Muneribus*, IX, no. 4, June 15, 1966. (can. 147).

287, § 2. *Politics and Labor Unions*. Clerics are permitted to engage in politics to the extent of exercising their rights as citizens, e.g., to vote. They are to engage actively in politics or in directing labor unions only when this is necessary for the defense of the rights of the Church or the common good, and this in the judgment of competent church authority.

289, § 1. *Military Service and Alien Civil Duties*. Clerics and candidates for sacred orders are forbidden to volunteer for armed military service unless they do so with the permission of their ordinary.

§ 2. The canon does not specify the public duties and civil offices alien to the clerical state. These can obviously vary with time and place and are thus subject to the determination of the ordinary. The present canon includes all such duties and offices that are forbidden to clerics by can. 285.

John Paul II, Vatican II, and the 1971 Synod of Bishops on the Ministerial Priesthood seem to be stronger than the canons above on the exclusion of secular activities and political action from priests and religious. The following are only a brief selection from the documents that could be adduced.

Secular Activity. The same synod, aware of modern problems, ideas and issues, gave the following norm: "In order to determine in concrete circumstances whether secular activity is in accord with the priestly ministry, inquiry should be made whether and in what way those duties and activities serve the mission of the Church, those who have not yet received the gospel message and finally the Christian community. This is to be judged by the local bishop with his presbyterium; and, if necessary, in consultation with the episcopal conference" (p. 20).

Political Activity. ". . . the priest, who is the witness of things to come, must keep a certain distance from any political office or involvement" (p. 21). "Leadership or active militancy on behalf of any political party is to be excluded by every priest unless, in concrete and exceptional circumstances, this is truly required by the good of the community, and receives the consent of the bishop after consultation with the priests' council and, if circumstances call for it, with the episcopal conference" (*ibid.*).

"Religious, for their part, should not exchange what is constitutive of their charism in the Church—total consecration to God, prayer, witness to the future life, pursuit of holiness—for political involvements that serve neither the religious themselves, since they lose their identity in the process, nor the Church, since she is impoverished by the loss of an essential dimension, nor the world and society, since they are deprived of the unique contribution that only religious can make to a legitimate pluralism" (John Paul II, *The Episcopal Office*, July 10, 1980, TPS, 26, 1981, pp. 72-3).

Funerals of Religious. Religious institutes may have their own cemetery. The funeral rites of religious are generally celebrated in their own church or oratory, by the superior if the institute is clerical, otherwise by the chaplain. Religious may choose another cemetery and church or oratory for the funeral rites, with the permission of its rector (cc. 1177, § 2; 1179; 1180, § 2; 1241).

The Apostolate of Institutes

673. *Most Effective Apostolic Action*. This is stated to be the testimony of the religious life; that is, actual sanctity of life, or the living of Christ as

perfectly as possible. It is to be fostered by prayer and penance. I do not believe that penance here means austerities but rather mortification. It is also to be remembered that the primary mortification should be passive; that is, the self-denial intrinsic to the acts of living Christ as perfectly as possible. Active mortification, that voluntarily chosen, such as fasting, also has its place in any Christian and more so in any religious life.

Canon 674 is important but it will be sufficiently clear from a mere reading.

675, § 1. *Apostolic Activity Appertains to the Nature of These Institutes.* Paul VI described the distinctive nature of the religious life, applicable to the total consecrated life, as "a state of life which keeps in view the constant growth of charity and its final perfection" (May 23, 1964; O'Connor, *Canon Law Digest*, VI, p. 427). The distinction of the consecrated life therefore is that it is the most helpful state of life to the attainment and fostering of charity. Sanctity, to which all are called, is principally the perfection of charity, which is defined by Royo Marin: "Charity is a theological virtue infused by God into the will by which we love God above all things for himself and ourselves and the neighbor for the love of God" (*Teologia della perfezione cristiana*, no. 254). It is not possible to love God without willing that he be loved and glorified by all creatures, which is the purpose of the apostolate. In the concrete, the perfection of love is to be lived in Christ our Lord, and in a personal, close, and especially total love of him. The primary charism of a religious member is to think, desire, and love as Christ, and he loved all men unto death. The apostolate is a duty that flows from love of God in itself and in Christ. It cannot therefore be considered as something extrinsic or harmful to this love. The apostolate in the apostolic institute is directly and immediately by apostolic acts, by the administration of the sacraments, preaching, teaching and instructing in the faith, and the spiritual and corporal works of mercy. In the contemplative, the apostolate is mediate and indirect, by witnessing to Christ, by austerity, and by prayer for the eternal, supernatural, and temporal life of mankind.

Logically, the first and second paragraphs state the conclusion of Vatican II, in PC, no. 8: "In such communities the very nature of the religious life requires apostolic action and services . . . Hence the entire religious life of the members of these communities should be penetrated by an apostolic spirit . . . their apostolic activity should result from an intimate union with Him. In this way it will happen that love for God and neighbor will itself be nurtured.''

§ 2. *Apostolic Mandate.* By its canonical erection as an institute of religious apostolic life, confirmed by the approval of the constitutions which necessarily contain these two basic elements, we have the following conclusions. The primary mandate of the institute is to live the religious life, to strive for the perfection of charity, as part of the Church. Fused with this is the mandate to go forth as apostles of the Church. Existence as officially religious and apostolic members comes from the Church and obviously, as the canon states, should be carried out in the name of and in union with the Church.

Apostolate of Religious in More Recent Documents. ''Christ, to be sure, gave his Church no proper mission in the political, economic, or social order. The purpose which he set before her is a religious one'' (GES, no. 42). The image that ecclesiastical documents draw of the religious is that the consuming function of the religious life is to strive for sanctity of life and consequently to labor for the sanctification of others. They make equally evident that the image of the priest is characterized by sanctity of life; his life is cultic, sacramental and pastoral— especially, with regard to both religious and priests, in favor of the poor and disadvantaged.

The 1971 Synod of Bishops on the Ministerial Priesthood gave the following norms for priests applicable also to religious: *''Secular Activity.* In order to determine in concrete circumstances whether secular activity is in accord with the priestly ministry, inquiry should be made whether and in what way those duties and activities serve the mission of the Church, those who have not yet received the gospel message and finally the Christian community. This is to be judged by the local bishop with his presbyterium and, if necessary, in consultation with the episcopal conference'' (p. 20). ''*Political Activity* . . . the priest, who is the witness of things to come, must keep a certain distance from political office or involvement. Leadership or active militancy on behalf of any political party is to be excluded by every priest unless, in concrete and exceptional circumstances, this is truly required by the good of the community, and receives the consent of the bishop after consultation with the priest's council and, if circumstances call for it, with the episcopal conference" (*ibid.*). "Secular duties and activities belong properly although not exclusively to the laymen" (GES, no. 43). "The laity must take on the renewal of the temporal order as their own special obligation" (AA, no. 7).

The Roman document on *Mutual Relations between Bishops and Religious* emphasizes that: religious must regard themselves as truly members of the diocesan family; exemption is not an obstacle to pastoral coordination and mutual good relations; the particular Church provides the historical place in which any given vocation finds its true expression and carries out its apostolic tasks; it is the particular and serious duty of religious to be attentive and docile to the magisterium; the episcopal ministry is the source of direction for the pastoral ministry of the entire people of God.

Religious priests must be said to belong to the clergy of the diocese; a new spirit of brotherhood and renewed bonds of collaboration are to be developed between the diocesan clergy and the religious communities; major superiors must be familiar with the apostolic needs of the dioceses in which their institute is called to work; a more substantial understanding among the religious institutes that work in the diocese is necessary; a very important place must be assigned to women in the pastoral activity of a diocese; the bishop must cultivate sincere and close relations with the superiors of religious men and women; and religious are to regard the bishop as the pastor of the entire diocese (see ℜfR, 39 [1980], pp. 105-14).

676-77. Only the following observations are opportune with regard to these canons.

677, § 1. *Special Purpose and Apostolic Works*. In its modern practice in approving constitutions, the SCRSI has characterized the striving for the perfection of charity as the sanctification of its members and as the general purpose of an institute; the contemplative aspect or particular apostolate as the distinctive way of living this general purpose and has termed it the special purpose. The Holy See has also demanded a determined special purpose, at least in lay institutes, and has not approved, except perhaps in mission countries, the undertaking of any work of the apostolate. The determined works must be submitted to the Holy See before the canonical erection as an institute of religious life. These works may not be added to in a general and permanent way without the approval of the Holy See, whether the institute is pontifical or diocesan (can. 583). They may be added to in a partial or temporary manner without such approval. It is evident that an institute should adapt its works according to the necessities of time and place.

It is equally evident that religious institutes may not enter a diocese with the intention of merely carrying out their own particular and isolated works. All such works must be attentively coordinated with the apostolate of the diocese in general and in particular matters. Otherwise the apostolate of the diocese would be disorganized, be more or less extensive in a particular matter and thoughtlessly neglected or exaggerated in other matters. Not merely "our apostolate" but the diocesan apostolate must be a more basic aspect of the apostolic mentality of religious.

678-83. These canons are on the highly important matter of the relations between diocesan bishops and religious institutes but they can be understood from a mere attentive reading.

CHAPTER IX

DEPARTURE AND DISMISSAL

Transfer to Another Religious Institute

684, § 1. *Definition*. Transfer is the leaving of a religious institute, in which one had made profession of perpetual public vows, and the immediate entrance, the vows remaining, into any other religious institute. Therefore, transfer is not verified in one who is only a novice or a professed of temporary vows, has received an indult of departure, or was dismissed from one and then applies for admission to another religious institute or autonomous monastery.

The study group voted explicitly to restrict transfer to religious of perpetual vows, which is equally the wording of can. 684, § 1. Consequently, a professed of temporary vows who wishes to transfer to another religious institute or autonomous monastery would secure an indult of departure, or leave the first institute at the expiration of this present temporary profession, and apply for admission to the second institute. He would be subject to all the canonical and proper laws on admission and probation as if he were originally entering the religious life. However, such a case could be presented to the Holy See for its decision and instructions while he is still in temporary vows in the first institute or autonomous monastery.

As stated in § 5, the passing to or from a religious to a secular institute or a society of apostolic life is a distinctive case. It requires the permission of the Holy See, whose instructions and norms specifically for this case, not those of can. 684-85, are to be followed.

A transfer is verified no matter what may be the nature of either or both religious institutes; namely, whether either or both are pontifical or diocesan, and also if the second is stricter as having more and greater austerities in such matters as abstinence, fasting, silence, cloister and nocturnal prayer.

Prudence. There is no doubt that solid reasons can exist for a transfer; e.g., a religious, either of apostolic or contemplative life, can be desirous of a sincere religious life but can be living in a deeply secularized institute or monastery. However, the suitability for *any* religious life of many who apply for a transfer is highly questionable, as is proved by their subsequent history. More than the usual care and investigation are to be exercised in accepting a transfer. This is more true in an autonomous monastery structure. The number of members of such a monastery is not only relatively small but they are also concentrated in one house. The effect of the trouble maker is proportionately concentrated and intensified. Any superior who ignores such norms of prudence, and it has often occurred, is simply adding a great obstacle to the happiness and consecrated living of his or her institute, and the obstacle is usually permanent.

Necessary Authorization and Process of Admission. The competent authorization in a centralized institute is the permission of the superior general with the deliberative vote of his council, of both the institute from which and to which the transfer is to be made. The process of a transfer begins with the fact that the member who wishes to transfer makes this known to his immediately higher superior and to the higher superior of the institute to which he wishes to transfer. As thorough an investigation as possible before entrance should be made of the suitability of the member for the life of the new institute. Ordinarily this is carried out by communication with his present local and higher superiors, who at times have not been too helpful nor conscious of their obligation to give an objective and complete description of the member's suitability for the religious life in general and for the life and work of the second institute.

Pre-entrance Probation. This is a very helpful means to ascertain without complications whether a candidate is suitable. It has often been used in recent years. For example, a candidate of an apostolic religious institute of sisters gets permission for a simple absence ("leave of absence") from her institute for at least a good part of the summer to observe and experiment with the contemplative monastery she wishes to enter. She can be occupied in such works in the monastery as helping an extern sister or can be brought fully into the monastery life, with the permission according to the existing universal and proper law on papal cloister. For example, the constitutions of the Discalced Carmelite Nuns, no. 102, read: "The prioress, with the consent of the chapter and of the proper ordinary, may allow a candidate to live in the monastery for a period of not more than three months, so that the community may find it easier to form a discerning judgment and the aspirant herself may realize what our life is really like." Towards the end of this period, the chapter or council would vote on the authorization to transfer.

§ 2. *Probation*. The candidate, if authorized to transfer, undergoes the probation of at least three years prescribed by § 2. The time and manner of the probation are to be determined in the constitutions or directory (§ 4). Other necessary determinations should be made by the immediate higher superior. This is not a formal noviceship and is therefore called a probation, not a noviceship.

Perpetual Profession. The voting of the admitting council should take place towards the end of the informal probation as to whether the candidate should be admitted to perpetual profession in the second institute, which is obviously the only profession to be made in the latter. The admitting higher superior and the specific vote of the council are the same as in the ordinary admission to perpetual profession. During or at the end of the probation the transferee may refuse to continue in or may be rejected by the second institute. The religious then returns to the first institute unless he has secured an indult of departure from the competent authority stated in can. 691.

§ 3. *Autonomous Monastery Transfer*. The exclusion of a professed of temporary vows from transferring by the Roman study group was absolute and therefore applies here also. Furthermore, if this were not true, there would be at least one new profession in the second institute, that of perpetual vows, which is contrary to the wording of this third paragraph. A transfer from one monastery to another of the same order, federation or confederation is one for which the consent of the major superior of each monastery and of the receiving chapter are required and sufficient. Neither a probation nor a new profession is required by canon law in this case. Evidently the existing requisites of proper law are to be observed.

One of these, in my judgment, should be an interval of at least two years before the consent of the receiving major superior and chapter becomes definitive and incorporates the transferee in the second monastery. Obviously this demands the repeated consent of the major superior and vote of the chapter. The "same order" was not a completely precise term in the past nor is it now. Monasteries are of the same order that follow the same Rule or constitutions and are called by the same name; for example, Visitandine nuns. The same definition would apply to a similar religious congregation; that is, a contemplative congregation of autonomous houses following the same Rule or constitutions.

685. *Effects of Transfer*. It is evident that this whole canon applies only when a new profession is made in the second institute. In a transfer from one monastery of the same order to another, a new profession is not required. The effects are evident in themselves from a mere reading of the canon.

Mixed Cases. Canon law distinguishes two types of transfers: (1) to another completely distinct institute, and (2) from one autonomous monastery to another of the same order, federation or confederation. The first is verified in such a transfer as that of a Redemptorist to the Passionists, a Jesuit to the Trappists, a Sister of Mercy to the Sisters of the Holy Child or to a Discalced Carmelite monastery, or a Discalced Carmelite nun to a Poor Clare monastery or to the Sisters of Mercy. The second case is verified in the transfer of a nun from one autonomous monastery to another of the same order; for example, from one Discalced Carmelite monastery to another.

If the transfer is from a centralized to an autonomous monastery structure (e.g., a Sister of Mercy becoming a Discalced Carmelite, or the opposite, e.g., a Carmelite nun becoming a Sister of Mercy) the competent authority remains the same. In the first case, the general superior of the Sisters of Mercy decides with the deliberative vote of her council and the major superior of the receiving monastery with the consent of its chapter. In the second case, the consent of the Carmelite monastery major superior, with the deliberative vote of her chapter or council, according to the proper constitutions, and the consent of the Mercy general superior with the deliberative vote of her council are required, because, as a transfer to a completely distinct institute, the norms of can. 684, § 1 must be followed.

Temporary Transfer in a Federation or Order of Monastic Structure. A temporary transfer has not even been mentioned in canon law but it exists in fact and is governed by the statutes of the federation or the constitutions of the order. The model statutes for federations of nuns (see RfR, 35 [1976], p. 99) require for such a transfer the consent of the chapters of the two monasteries of the federation; the favorable opinion of the president and of the religious assistant of the federation; and the free consent of the religious (see nos. 81, 87). The Discalced Carmelite constitutions require the consent of the chapters of both monasteries of the order, the free consent of the religious, and also the consent of the Holy See for a transfer of more than three years. This transfer is from one monastery to another of the same Carmelite order (nos. 146-7).

Voluntary and Imposed Exclaustration

686, § 1. *Competent Authority for Voluntary Exclaustration.* The general superior, with the consent of his or her council, may grant an indult of exclaustration to a professed of perpetual vows, for a serious reason, but not beyond three years. If the member is a cleric, the previous consent of the ordinary of the place of the exclaustrated residence must be had. Serious reasons are required. These have been commonly given as sufficient reasons: a business undertaking, care of personal health, and care or support of one's parents, as likewise others of similar import.

The canons do not say that exclaustration may not be used if a simple absence would suffice.

To give or prolong an indult beyond three years is reserved to the Holy See or, if the institute is diocesan, to the diocesan bishop. The Holy See alone is competent to grant any exclaustration to a nun (§ 2). The religious requests the indult in voluntary exclaustration and is not obliged to use it after it has been granted. It is the practice to make such a petition to the Holy See or a diocesan bishop through a higher superior, who should give his or her opinion, substantiated by pertinent reasons and facts, as to whether the indult should be granted. These same formalities should be observed by a lower superior in a petition to the general superior.

§ 3. *Imposed Exclaustration.* This demands the petition of the general superior with the consent of his or her council. It may be imposed by the Holy See on a religious of a pontifical institute and by the diocesan bishop on a religious of a diocesan institute. The reasons must be serious, and equity and charity are to be observed. Imposed exclaustration, often called exclaustration at the will of the Holy See, originated in the practice of the SCRSI. The essential characteristics of this exclaustration are that it is imposed, is of obligation, and is a precept of dwelling outside the institute. The reason is frequently the good of the community; i.e., the conduct of the religious is a source of serious harm to the institute. Often the good of the member is also intended; i.e., for his own good he should be exclaustrated. Typical cases are of those who are notably deficient in observance or obedience and especially members who for a variety of reasons must be classed as very difficult to live with. In actual life they are readily discernible. The effects of voluntary exclaustration (see can. 687) apply also to imposed exclaustration.

These cases were said to be of greater frequency in institutes of women. They are often accompanied by physical or mental maladies. The member is obliged to work for his own support, but the institute has an obligation in charity to support him insofar as he cannot do so himself. As understood in the past, this exclaustration is not imposed for any definite period of time but it is not perpetual. It lasts as long as the reasons and purposes persist in the judgment of the SCRSI or the diocesan bishop in the case of a religious of a diocesan institute, who alone may permit the member to be received back in the community.

The canon demands only serious reason—no warnings, no admonitions with a threat of dismissal or imposed exclaustration, and no number of violations. My own experience is that such members can practically always be judged as permanent problems. The canons impose no such obligation, but I would counsel that the member be granted the right of free written defenses against the charges of the institute. This practice would also aid the competent authority to make his decision.

687. An exclaustrated member is freed only of the religious obligations incompatible with his new condition of life. He remains under the care and dependence of superiors and, especially if he is a cleric, of the local ordinary. He may wear the habit, unless the indult states the contrary, but he lacks both active and passive voice (see also can. 665, § 1).

Leaving and Exclusion at the End of a Temporary Profession

689, § 1. *Exclusion is Merely Non-Admission.* In this can. 689, § 1 we have the continuation of a specific canon on the exclusion from a religious institute as distinguished from a dismissal—even though it is evident that a non-admission to first temporary profession without a prolongation of the noviceship, a simple non-admission to a renewal of temporary vows, and a non-admission to perpetual profession without a prolongation of temporary vows of themselves constitute an exclusion from an institute effective at the end of the present temporary profession. Exactly this is stated in can. 657, § 1: "On the expiration of the time for which a profession had been made, a religious who voluntarily requests it and is judged suitable shall be admitted to the renewal of the profession or to perpetual profession; otherwise he is to leave."

It is evident also from this canon that the competent higher superior for exclusion is identified with the one competent for admission to the further profession. Canons 656 and 658 require at least the consultative vote of the competent higher superior's council for admission to any

temporary or perpetual profession, as does can. 689 for exclusion. Just
what is gained by the addition of can. 689? This matter has therefore
been explained above in can. 607, as also in can. 641 on refusal of a
vocation, and also in the canon quoted above, 657, § 1. We shall
consequently give here only summations and explanations that will be
helpful when the aspect of non-admission, or exclusion, is being
considered.

§ 2. *Sufficient Reasons for Exclusion*. Evidently the sufficient
reasons are those that render a member certainly unsuited or only
dubiously suited for admission to the profession in question. It is permitted but not obligatory to grant a renewal or prolongation of temporary
vows in the dubious case provided there is solid hope that certain
suitability will be attained by the renewal or prolongation. Canon law
expresses the principle of suitability by demanding merely just, not
serious or grave, reasons for an exclusion. In judging the sufficiency of
the reasons, the common good of the institute is to be considered above
that of the individual. The following are the particular reasons usually
listed by authors by way of example: the lack of a vocation to the
religious life or of a firm and constant vocation; serious doubts as to the
general suitability of the person for the religious life or that of the
particular institute; ineptitude for the work of the institute, even if fully
known before the profession, whether the ineptitude arises from a lack of
general ability, intelligence or application, or from a defect of prudent
judgment, laziness, negligence, or from culpable or inculpable causes; if
it is foreseen that the member will be only mediocre, will be tepid,
careless in the spiritual life, or wordly; those who are habitually negli-
gent, careless or tepid in religious observance, even though not in serious
matters, and who have refused to correct their conduct; those who cause
serious discord in the community; those who will find community life
very difficult and/or will make it difficult for others; and when it is
foreseen that the subject will be harmful rather than useful to the
institute. An exclusion without a just and reasonable cause is a sin
against charity and the law of the Church but it is not unjust nor invalid.

Exclusion in an Institute of Only Temporary Vows. In the very few institutes that had only temporary vows or in which the prescribed duration of temporary profession was longer than six years, it was the more probable and common opinion that after more than six years in temporary vows merely just and reasonable causes did not suffice for exclusion but serious and culpable reasons were necessary. The arguments for this opinion were that can. 642, § 2 appeared to liken a temporary profession beyond six years to perpetual vows and that it seemed inequitable to exclude one who had been so long in religion for merely just and reasonable causes. This same opinion is still probable, but this matter may be determined in the proper and approved law of the institute.

Ill Health. A physical or psychic infirmity, even if contracted after profession, that in the judgment of experts renders a subject unsuitable for living the life of an institute, is a sufficient cause for exclusion, unless the infirmity was contracted through the negligence of the institute or work performed in it (can. 689, § 2).

Manifestation of Reasons. The member is to be informed of his exclusion in due time, orally or in writing, by the competent higher superior personally or through another. Kindness is to be shown to the excluded member. Canon law does not oblige the competent higher superior to manifest the reasons for the exclusion to the excluded member. This may be done, and some authors counsel it that the religious may institute a recourse to a higher superior or to the Holy See, if he chooses to do so. The reasons should always be drawn up completely and accurately and retained in the files of the institute that a reply may be given in the event of a recourse, particularly of one to the Holy See. It would also seem strange to almost anyone that a member would be excluded after several years in the religious life without being given the reasons.

Recourse. Canon law says nothing about a recourse against an exclusion. The one excluded may institute a recourse to a higher superior or the Holy See but it does not have a suspensive effect. The person remains excluded also while the recourse is pending. A recourse to the sacred congregation has little hope of success unless the exclusion can be clearly proved to have been unfounded. The member should leave the institute and put off the habit. He may be permitted to remain in a house of the institute and to wear the habit until the recourse is definitively settled.

Effects of a Voluntary Departure and of Exclusion. The vows and all consequent rights and obligations cease at the expiration of the present temporary profession.

Departure Before Expiration. If serious reasons so demand, superiors may permit a member to leave some days before the expiration of the vows provided he puts off the habit and intends to observe the vows until the expiration date, e.g., because of the embarrassment or difficulties that his continued presence would cause. If required by an urgent reason, an earlier departure may be permitted, e.g., of two or three weeks.

Voluntary Departure

688, § 2; 691. This was formerly called secularization. It occurs during the time of vows, temporary or perpetual, and thus differs from a voluntary leaving at the expiration of a temporary profession. It is voluntary and in this way differs from a dismissal, which occurs during vows but not because of the voluntary petition of a member. It is now apparently called an indult of departure. In popular language indults of this kind are called a dispensation from the vows. Departure is a voluntary leaving of the religious institute by which a member is separated completely from membership in the institute and freed completely of all vows, as also of all rights and obligations that have their source in religious profession. By this departure the member ceases to be a member.

1. *Competent Authority.* For one in temporary vows, the competent authority in any religious institute is the general superior with the consent of his council. Presumably in an autonomous house or monastery, this authority is the local major superior with the consent of the chapter or council, according to proper law. In a diocesan institute and an autono-

mous monastery defined in can. 615, for validity the indult must be confirmed by the bishop of the assigned house of the religious. For a member in perpetual vows: in a pontifical institute, the right to grant this indult appertains to the Holy See; in a diocesan institute, it may be granted also by the diocesan bishop of the assigned house of the religious.

2. *Sufficient Reasons.* Serious and, for a professed of perpetual vows, even most serious reasons are required for departure. The ecclesiastical authority competent to grant the indult is the judge of their sufficiency. There must be a reason over and above the mere desire to leave the institute. The most common reason is that the member finds the institute life morally impossible or too difficult, even if this state arises from culpable causes that he will not correct. The difficulty may have its source in the vow of chastity, poverty or obedience, the community life, work, or general life of the institute. A reason insufficient in itself may become sufficient when the mental state of the member that he will not correct is taken into account—for example, if his desire to leave makes him useless or a source of harm to the institute. Other reasons of equal or greater import will suffice—for example, lack of suitability for the work of the institute, mental depression, necessary support of parents, and the case of those who are counseled to leave because otherwise the institute will initiate their dismissal.

3. *Petition.* The member himself asks for the indult of departure, since it is a voluntary leaving of the institute. He is to write out or at least sign his request, stating his name in religious and secular life, name of his institute, province, his present address, age, number of years in the institute, of what vows he is professed and for how long, that he voluntarily requests an indult of departure, all his reasons, and the date. A petition to the Holy See or the diocesan bishop for a professed of perpetual vows is to be forwarded through the general superior with his own vote and that of his council on whether the member should depart. The general superior should enclose a letter with the petition giving all information and facts pertinent to the case. At least ordinarily, the same process should be followed by a local or provincial superior in forward-

ing a petition to the general superior for a professed of temporary vows.

4. *Cleric Petitioner*. The indult of departure is not granted before the cleric has found a bishop who will incardinate him in his diocese or receive him at least experimentally. If received in the latter way, he is incardinated in the diocese by law itself on the completion of five years of experimentation, unless the bishop has rejected him (can. 693).

5. *Notification and Rejection*. An indult of departure legitimately granted accompanied by the notification of the member, unless it was rejected by the member himself in the act of notification, effects by law itself dispensation from the vows and from all obligations arising from profession. The two requisites are notification and the absence of rejection in the notification. In an oral presentation, which should be followed by a written statement of the contents of the indult, two witnesses are to attest in the record of the notification and the absence of rejection. When the notification is by mail, a written receipt of the reception of the letter should be secured. The separated member should be given in writing a dated and signed statement on the stationery of the institute that he had received an indult of departure from the institute and accordingly had left the institute free of all obligations of the religious life (can. 692).

690. *Readmission After Departure*. One who legitimately left an institute on the completion of the noviceship or after any temporary profession of religious vows may be readmitted to the same institute, without the obligation (which, however, may be imposed) of repeating the noviceship, by the general superior with the consent of his council. The same superior determines the appropriate probation as to duration and manner before temporary profession and the duration of the temporary vows to precede perpetual profession but according to the norms of cann. 655 and 657. Can. 655 requires that temporary profession be not less than three nor longer than six years. Only in a prolongation may it be extended to nine years. The second paragraph of can. 690 explicitly states that the superior of an autonomous monastery with the consent of his council enjoys the same faculty.

This favor does not extend to one who left after perpetual profession. The reasons are: (1) this was the sense of the same previous law, and there is no indication of an intention of extending the favor; (2) and the order of the words, "completion of the noviceship or after profession." All possibility of doubt in this matter might have been removed by phrasing the canon: "or after any temporary profession . . . "

694, § 1. *Dismissal by Law*. A member is automatically, ipso facto, by law itself dismissed who has notoriously given up the Catholic faith or has contracted or attempted marriage, even merely civilly. The dismissal is effected by law itself, without any decree or act of a superior or Church authority, and at the instant that either of the two specified acts is committed.

Subject. The subject of this dismissal is any professed religious, man or woman, of perpetual or temporary vows. A novice is not the subject but the commission of either crime is evidently more than a sufficient reason for his dismissal by the competent major superior.

1° *Notoriously Falling Away From the Faith*. A notorious crime has been defined as one actually and commonly known, e.g., in the religious house, and committed in such circumstances that both the fact of the commission and the imputability of the perpetrator are certain and evident. Can. 751 states: "Heresy is tenacious denial or doubt after baptism of a truth that is to be held with divine and Catholic faith; apostasy is the repudiation of the total Christian faith; schism is refusal of obedience to the supreme pontiff or of communion with members of the Church who are obedient to him."

The first cause of dismissal by law is "falling away from the faith." Schism therefore is not included. It is not in itself an act against faith but obedience nor does it necessarily imply a denial of faith. The two acts that here effect dismissal are apostasy and heresy, also if either is associated with schism. Apostasy is a denial or a positive doubt about the entire Christian faith, e.g., the existence of God, the fact or possibility of Christian revelation or of the supernatural order. The canon does not demand that the religious have joined a non-Christian church, e.g., Judaism, Buddhism, Islam. A positive doubt is had when the intellect judges that there are sufficient reasons for affirming and denying the proposition, that the reasons on neither side are convincing, and therefore suspends assent to the proposition. In a negative doubt the intellect suspends assent because it does not perceive reasons for affirming or denying the proposition. This is to be classed rather as ignorance. As in heresy, a positive doubt is sufficient for apostasy. Heresy is the denial or positive doubt about one or some dogmas of faith, which are doctrines taught infallibly by the Church.

2° *Contracting or Attempting Marriage, Even Only Civilly.* This act is the contracting (validly) or the attempting (invalidly) of marriage by any type of Catholic or non-Catholic ceremony, or merely civil act, provided both parties gave a naturally valid consent. The form of celebration of a civil marriage must be valid according to the civil law of the place of celebration. The offense presupposes a marriage consent valid from the natural law and is not verified if the consent is vitiated in either party by an essential defect, e.g., ignorance, simulation, physical violence, or grave fear. However, it is to be presumed that true consent was given, and this presumption is sufficient to declare the religious dismissed. In itself the invalidity of the marriage does not exclude the offense—i.e., the offense is still verified if the marriage is invalid because it was attempted outside the Church or due to a diriment impediment. In virtue of can. 1088, a public perpetual vow of chastity in a religious institute is a diriment impediment to marriage and thus, unless dispensed, invalidates marriage.

§ 2. *Effects and Declaration of Fact.* The effects of a dismissal by law, since it is a legitimate dismissal, are the same as for any other legitimate dismissal. The canon commands the higher superior with the consultative vote of his council, without delay, to make a declaration of fact concerning the offense. Some institutes restrict this right to the general superior; some also demand a deliberative vote of the council. The declaration is to be made by the superior of an autonomous monastery, with the advice or consent of the chapter or council according to proper law. The declaration of fact is merely a description of the pertinent points of the case, the headings of the proof, any documentary evidence, and the conclusion that the religious was dismissed by canon law. The declaration and proofs are to be retained in the secret files of the higher superior who made the declaration. The purpose of the declaration is to possess proof of the dismissal by law for any eventuality that may arise in the future.

695, § 1. *Obligatory Dismissal.* A religious should be dismissed because of the following crimes: homicide, abduction, mutilation, serious wounding (can. 1397); procuring of abortion (can. 1398); clerical concubinage and a cleric remaining in other external sexual sins (can. 1395, § 1). However, the dismissal is not obligatory in the cases of can. 1395, § 1 if the superior believes it is not absolutely necessary and that the emendation of the member, the restitution of justice and reparation of scandal can be sufficiently attained by other means.

§ 2. *Dismissal Procedure.* The major superior collects the proofs of the fact and imputability of the crime (see can. 1321, § 3), informs the delinquent member of the accusation and the proofs; and also informs him of his right of defending himself.

All acts are to be signed by a major superior and a notary and, with the replies of the member reduced to writing and signed by the member himself, transmitted to the general superior, who then follows the procedure of cc. 699-700.

696. § 1. *Causes for the Ordinary Dismissal.* A member may also be dismissed for other serious, external, culpable, and juridically proved reasons, such as habitual neglect of the obligations of the consecrated life, repeated violations of the sacred bonds, obstinate disobedience to the legitimate orders of superiors in grave matter, serious scandal arising from the culpable conduct of the member, obstinate defense or diffussion of doctrines condemned by the magisterium of the Church, public adherence to ideologies infected with materialism or atheism, the illegitimate absence described in can. 665, § 2 and protracted for six months, and other reasons of similar gravity that may be determined in proper law: e.g., exciting other members to insubordination, causing dissension and factions in the community, defamation of the institute or its members among seculars, drunkenness and drug addiction.

§ 2. *Lesser Reasons for Professed of Temporary Vows.* Lesser reasons listed in proper law suffice for the dismissal of a professed of temporary vows. Inasmuch as these members are still in a state of probation, inculpable reasons are necessarily also sufficient for their dismissal, e.g., a lack of aptitude for the religious, community or apostolic life of the institute. For example, it is an evident fact of experience that a lack of intellectual capacity often clearly manifests itself only after the noviceship and in studies. Inculpable reasons sufficed under the preceding canon law but such reasons are in no way indicated in the present canon law (see the present can. 19). While can. 689, § 2 refers only to an exclusion from further profession because of ill health, it may from the reasoning above be applied also to the dismissal of professed of temporary vows. It is evidently a lack of aptitude for the life of the institute. Furthermore, there is no canon that forbids their dismissal because of ill health as the former can. 647, § 2, 2°.

697. *Dismissal Process.* In the cases given under the preceding canon, whether the professed is of perpetual or temporary vows, and if the major superior, with the advice of his or her council, judges that the dismissal process is to be initiated, the following are to be done:

1° The major superior is to collect or complete the proofs.

2° He is in writing or before two witnesses to admonish the member, with an explicit threat of a dismissal that will follow unless he comes to a right mind. He is to state clearly the reason for dismissal and to give the member the full opportunity of defending himself. If this admonition is in vain, he is to proceed to a second admonition after an interval of at least fifteen days. The explicit threat of dismissal must never be omitted. The essential notes of an admonition are three: the major superior reprehends the member for the violation(s) already committed, warns him to avoid such conduct in the future, and adds an explicit threat of dismissal if the member should not desist from such conduct. Other measures that the particular case demands for the avoidance of future violations are to be employed by the superior. Almost necessarily this will imply putting the member under the vigilance of the local superior. Other means can be the changing of the work or location of the offender and, in general, the removal or lessening of the occasions of a future violation.

3° If the second admonition also is ineffective and the major superior, with the advice of his council, judges that there is sufficient certainty of the incorrigibility of the member and of the deficiencies of the defenses, after fifteen days have elapsed without effect since the last admonition, all the acts, signed by the major superior and a notary along with the responses of the member signed by the member, are to be transmitted to the general superior. Although this is not so clear in the canons, the responses of the member should be given to the major superior after each admonition and the subsequent violation. He should be allowed sufficient time to prepare his defenses. In the dismissal of a professed of temporary vows for inculpable causes, numbers 2 and 3 obviously do not apply, and the decision of the major superior is to be transmitted, with pertinent proofs, to the general superior after the discussion of the matter with the council.

698. *Free Communication with the General Superior*. In all cases of can. 695-6, the member always retains the right of free communication with the general superior, to whom also he may directly give his defenses.

699, § 1. *Collegial Decision of the General Superior and Council*. In a purely collegial act the decision appertains to the whole body, superior and council, as such. An absolute majority is required for a decision to dismiss (e.g., three out of five), and the general superior must follow the decision. For the validity of the decision, the council must consist of at least four actual members—thus, with the superior, constituting at least five members. They are to proceed collegially in weighing accurately the proofs, reasons for the dismissal, and the defenses. The decision for dismissal must be by secret vote and have attained at least an absolute majority. Again for the validity of the decree of dismissal, it must contain at least summarily the motives in law and fact on which it rests.

§ 2. *Autonomous Monasteries*. In these monasteries as defined in can. 615, the dismissal appertains to the diocesan bishop, to whom the superior is to submit the acts examined by the council. The canon does not demand this but it seems to me that the bishop should be given the result of a secret vote of the superior and council on the dismissal.

700. *Confirmation of Decree of Dismissal*. The decree of dismissal is not

effective, in a pontifical institute, until it is confirmed by the Holy See, to which the decree and all acts are to be submitted. For a diocesan institute, this confirmation appertains to the diocesan bishop of the house to which the member is attached.

Recourse. In a dismissal of a member of an autonomous monastery issued by the diocesan bishop (can. 699, § 2) or the dismissal of a member of a diocesan institute, which is confirmed by the diocesan bishop (can. 700), the decree of dismissal, for its validity, must contain mention of the right of the dismissed member to recur, with suspensive effect, to the competent authority within ten days from the acceptance of notification of the decree of dismissal. The member may recur after the ten days but this recourse does not suspend the effect of the decree of dismissal. The canon literally says the same thing about the dismissal of a member of a pontifical institute, since it makes no exception for this type of institute and its wording is universal, even though in this case the Holy See had both examined the reasons of the dismissed member against the decree and had itself confirmed the decree.

701. *Effects of Dismissal.* As soon as the decree of dismissal is effective, the religious vows cease, as do all rights and obligations arising from religious profession. If the member is a cleric, he may not exercise sacred orders until he finds a bishop who will receive him, after an appropriate probation, in his diocese, according to the norm of can. 693 or at least permit the exercise of sacred orders.

702. *No Compensation for Work.* Any recompense that a religious receives for his work is acquired for his institute. The statement of the canon that a religious may not make any claim of compensation for work performed in the institute is therefore evident. It has been the past practice, at least in apostolic lay institutes, that candidates on their entrance would sign a statement, attested by two religious witnesses, that they would not make any claim for any work in the institute if they left or were dismissed. This practice may be maintained without the necessity of including it as a matter of proper law. The principle of no compensation was understood in fact and in the statement to apply also to the time

of the postulancy and noviceship. On its part the institute assumed the obligation of the support of the religious for the time he remained in the institute.

The canon commands an institute to observe equity and charity toward a separated member. Unless the former member can provide for himself or herself, he should be given suitable clothing, personal effects, and a sum of money to enable him to return home becomingly and to provide him with the means of a respectable livelihood for a reasonable length of time. According to the needs of the individual, the institute should interest itself effectively in the spiritual, moral, social and temporal welfare of those separated from the institute, assisting them in fitting themselves into the social and working secular life.

703. *Provisional Sending Back to Secular Life.* The subject of this provisional return is any professed religious, man or woman, and professed of perpetual or temporary vows. As soon as the return is decided, the religious leaves the institute. The return is not a dismissal and does not produce the effects of a dismissal, but the preceding paragraph is to be applied to such a member. The competent authority specified below decides for or against initiating dismissal or refers the matter in a full report to the Apostolic See.

Reasons Required. The reason must be either of the following:

(1) *Grave External Scandal.* This is a culpable defamatory act, committed within or outside the religious house, which is well known outside the house or known only to a few externs who will not keep the matter secret; for example, a sin against good morals.

(2) *Very Serious Imminent Harm to the Institute.* This is an extraordinary injury or harm certainly and proximately threatening, at least reductively, not merely one or some individuals but the religious house, province, or institute. The religious must be the cause of this harm but it is not certain that he must be a culpable cause. Examples of this reason are the proximate judicial accusation of a defamatory crime in either the moral or political order; sexual actions with students when it is foreseen that these will become public and bring infamy to the house, province or

institute; a serious threat to set the house on fire or against the life of the superior or another member of the institute; and a serious loss of temporal property of the house, province or institute.

Three conditions are required in both cases. Since such an extraordinary action should not be taken against a religious because of mere probability, conjecture or suspicion, the existence of the cause must be certain; it must also be impossible to avoid the scandal or harm in other ways, for example, by transferring the religious to another house; and there must be at least probability that the scandal or harm can be averted or appreciably diminished by the provisional return to secular life or, in the language of the canon, by his immediate ejection from the religious house.

The competent authority for deciding such a return is ordinarily the major superior. In prudence and if practically possible, a provincial should refer the case to the general superior or at least consult the latter. In an autonomous monastery, the competent authority is the local major superior. In a more urgent case in which the time necessary for a recourse to the general or provincial superior would imperil the avoidance of the scandal or injury or of its continuance, the competent authority is the local superior with the consent of his council or, if the circumstances demand it, the local superior alone.

704. *Reporting Those in any way Separated From the Institute.* This would include those who have obtained an indult of departure, left or were excluded at the end of a temporary profession, the dismissed, the provisionally returned to secular life and those who left the institute without permission or with permission but remained away from it without permission, and any similar cases. Such members are to be listed in the report on the state of the institute to the Holy See. (see can. 592, § 1)

705-6. *Religious Promoted to the Episcopal or Similar Dignities.* The first canon will be clear from a mere reading. The particular churches likened to a diocese are a territorial prelature and abbey, an apostolic vicariate and prefecture, a stably erected apostolic administration, as also a personal prelature.

If by his religious profession such a member has lost the right to retain and acquire the proprietorship of temporal goods for himself, he has the use, usufruct and administration of such goods that come to him personally, but their proprietorship appertains to the diocese or particular church. Other dignitaries, namely those that are not at the head of a particular church, acquire such property for their institute or, if the institute is not capable of proprietorship, for the Holy See.

The sense of the other two numbers of this canon is evident from a mere reading, as also that of the following three canons, 707-9.

CHAPTER X

COMPUTATION OF TIME

The following are examples of at least the principal matters in the religious life on which a computation of time occurs.

Days. An election must be accepted within eight days (can. 177, § 1), as also the petitioning of the confirmation of an election (can. 179, § 1), the sending of a postulation (can. 182, § 1), and for one postulated to accept an admitted postulation (can. 188, § 2). Ten days are granted for the suspensive recourse against a decree of dismissal (can. 700). "In law a day is understood as the space of twenty-four hours counted continuously, and it begins from midnight, unless expressly established otherwise . . . " (can. 202, § 1). Therefore, if any of the acts listed above occurred on June 1, at 10 a.m., the remaining part of June 1 is not computed. The computation of the eight days for acceptance of the election begins at midnight of June 1-2 and ends at midnight of June 9-10. If a member was dismissed on the same day and hour, the ten days for the suspensive recourse end at midnight of June 11-12. "Useful time is understood to be that which is at the disposal of a person for the exercise or prosecution of his right so that, if the person is ignorant of his right or incapable of acting, this time does not run" (can. 201, § 2). In all the examples given above, the time is useful time. The opposite is continuous time, in which there is no interruption (can. 201, § 1).

Age. The 17, 18 and 21 complete years required for entrance into the noviceship, temporary and perpetual profession (cc. 643, §1,1°; 656, 1°; 658, 1°).

Period of One or Several Weeks, Months or Years, in which is included the 12 months of noviceship (can. 648, § 1), "if continuous" (can. 202, § 2). The norm for such cases is can. 203, which reads as follows:

"§ 1. The beginning day is not computed in the term, unless this beginning coincides with the beginning of the day or *it is otherwise expressly established in law.*

" § 2. *Unless the contrary is established*, the final day is computed in the term, which, if the term consists of one or many months or years, one or many weeks, is finished with the completion of the last day of this number, or if the month lacks a day of the same number, with the completion of the final day of that month."

If one is born at 10 a.m. on June 1, 1980, the remaining part of the first day, June 1, is not computed, and the computation begins at midnight of June 1-2. The last day is computed, so that one is 17 only at midnight of June 1-2, 1997, and 18 and 21 only at the same day and hour of 1998 and 2001. A continuous 12 months of noviceship begun on the same day and hour is completed at midnight of June 1-2, 1981. This is the canonical norm and the one to be followed unless the contrary is established in common or proper law.

In a second year or additional six months of noviceship, which are not prescribed by canon law, the computation of time does not have to be made according to the canonical norm. A novice, in a two-year noviceship, who begins the noviceship on the same day and hour, finished the first year at midnight of June 1-2, 1981, but may make the first profession on June 1, 1982.

"203, § 1, *it is otherwise established in law.*" This exceptive clause was not contained in the 1917 code (see can. 34, § 3, 3°). We shall take the same example of one born at 10 a.m. on June 1, 1980. According to the canonical norm above, the remaining part of this June 1, the first day, is not computed, and the computation begins at midnight of June 1-2. A religious institute may establish a contrary norm according to the exceptive clause quoted above, so that the first day will be computed and the duration begins at midnight of May 31-June 1 and ends at midnight of May 31-June 1, or, what is the same thing, at the beginning of June 1,

1997, as also 18 and 21 on the same day and hour of 1998 and 2001. A continuous 12 months of noviceship begun on the same day and hour is completed also at the beginning of June 1, 1981.

"203 § 2, *Unless the contrary is established.*" This clause is exceptive to the canonical norm of requiring the completion of the last day of the duration. Therefore, the proper law of a religious institute may establish that the last day has only to be begun, not finished. If one is born on June 1, 1980, he is 17 years of age at midnight of May 31-June 1, or what is the same thing, at the beginning of June 1, 1997.

I would suggest that the first exceptive norm be adopted for the proper law of a religious institute, which would read: "in a period of one or several weeks, months or years, e.g., in age, continuous 12 months of noviceship, duration of temporary professions and of the office of superiors, the first day is computed and the duration attained at the beginning of the last day of the same number."

Duration of Office of Superiors. Expiration and Renewal of Temporary Profession and the Making of the Perpetual Profession.

If a novice made the first temporary profession of vows for three years on June 1, 1980, or a member was elected general superior for a six-year term on the same day and hour, the profession and term would expire at midnight of June 1-2, 1983 and 1986 respectively, according to the 1917 code. This agrees with the present canonical norm of can. 203. However, the 1917 code permitted the renewal of temporary vows, the making of perpetual profession, and the next election at any time on the recurrence the same day, i.e., on June 1, 1983 and 1986, even though this could be done only on June 2 according to the then and present canonical norms in themselves, which demand the completion of the final day of June 1. The 1917 code was thus giving a concession. However, if the suggestion given above is followed of computing the first day in the duration of professions and term of office, the last day of the duration will again be attained at midnight of May 31-June 1; or, what is the same thing, at the beginning of June 1. The same effect could be accomplished by legislating that the last day, June 1, need not be completed but only begun. The only disadvantage I see with this new system is that a religious will be without vows from midnight until the profession is made on the last day, June 1.

Broken Noviceship. There cannot be a broken religious profession or superiorship. The vows and office remain for the full time of the particular profession or designation. They can be terminated, not broken. The 12 months of noviceship now prescribed for validity by canon law can be broken by absences for apostolic activity or other reasons. Non-continuous, interrupted or broken time is computed according to can. 202, § 1, in which a month is defined as a period of 30 days. Therefore, 12 months are 360 days. The canon does not say for a year, which is defined by the same canon as a space of 365 days.

INDEX